Pope's
DUNCIAD
of 1728

Pope's DUNCIAD of 1728

A History and Facsimile

DAVID L· VANDER MEULEN

Published for the
BIBLIOGRAPHICAL SOCIETY
OF THE UNIVERSITY OF VIRGINIA
and THE NEW YORK PUBLIC LIBRARY
by the UNIVERSITY PRESS OF VIRGINIA

Charlottesville and London
1991

THE UNIVERSITY PRESS OF VIRGINIA
Copyright © 1991 by the Rector and Visitors
of the University of Virginia

First published 1991

Library of Congress Cataloging-in-Publication Data

Pope, Alexander, 1688–1744.
[Dunciad]
Pope's Dunciad of 1728 : a history and facsimile / David L. Vander
Meulen.
p.   cm.
Includes bibliographical references.
ISBN 0–8139–1268–7
1. Pope, Alexander, 1688–1744. Dunciad—Criticism, Textual.
I. Vander Meulen, David L.   II. Title.
PR3625.A1   1990
821'.5—dc20   90–30426
                                                                                            CIP

Typography, decorations, and binding design by Warren Chappell
Composition by Graphic Composition of Athens, Georgia
Printing by Malloy Lithographing, Inc., Ann Arbor, Michigan
Binding by John Dekker & Sons, Inc., Grand Rapids, Michigan

Printed in the United States of America

To
MY PARENTS
as Pope would wish

Contents

Foreword by Lola L. Szladits / ix
Preface / xi
Abbreviations / xvii

The History of Pope's DUNCIAD, 1728

The Work / 3
The Edition / 29
The Copy / 41
The Annotations / 47
Works Cited / 65

THE DUNCIAD of 1728: A Facsimile

73

Appendixes

1. Collation of the Authorized 1728 Impressions / 143
2. The Texts of the Unauthorized Editions of 1728 / 156
3. Varieties and States of the Altar Frontispiece / 161
4. The 1728 Advertisement for *The Progress of Dulness* / 164
5. Annotations in the 1728 Huntington *Dunciad* / 166

Index

171

Foreword

THE *DUNCIAD* OF 1728, though today much sought after by collectors and all but impossible to obtain, is an unprepossessing little pamphlet of fifty-two pages, bearing no author's name." So wrote Maynard Mack in his definitive biography of Alexander Pope in 1985. The bibliopolic frenzy surrounding this slim item is well attested by auction records of this century, just as the vehement debates over its bibliographical complications have been duly enshrined in scholarly publications. But despite such interest, the work itself has been accessible only to specialists. The present book makes it available to a wider audience.

The copy reproduced here is the one in which Jonathan Richardson, Jr. (1694–1771), recorded his collations of an early manuscript of the poem. Both it and a 1736 edition, in which Richardson registered the readings of a later holograph, are now in the Berg Collection of English and American Literature of the New York Public Library. Richardson and his father, a portrait painter of the same name (1665–1745), were lifelong friends of Pope who also collaborated in literary productions of their own. The collations the son undertook were at the behest of Pope himself; in gratitude, Pope presented him with many of his literary manuscripts.

Habent sua fata libelli, and it is not totally by accident that this unique item reached the Berg Collection. The Library acquired the volume in 1941 as part of the peerless collection of Owen D. Young (1874–1962), who apparently bought it from

Foreword

an English dealer in the 1920s but who left no record of its provenance. It thus joined what has now become a group of about one hundred and fifty early editions of Pope—a collection that ranks only about tenth in the number of such items but stands at the forefront in their significance. On the shelves surrounding this book are such volumes as the only known fine-paper copies of *An Essay on Criticism* (1711) and *The Rape of the Lock* (1714), the latter presented by Pope to Mrs. Elizabeth Fortescue; the first volume of Pope's collected *Works* (1717), which he gave to Jonathan Richardson, Sr.; the second volume of his *Works* (1735), inscribed to Jonathan Swift; his collected prose *Works* (1737), a gift to Robert Arbuthnot; and one of only two known copies of Pope's edition of the posthumous works of William Wycherley, volume 2 (1729)—stitched, uncut, and in the original wrappers.

The Berg Collection is pleased to join with the Bibliographical Society of the University of Virginia in making conveniently available the text and David Vander Meulen's history of this classic exposure of cultural folly.

LOLA L. SZLADITS
Curator, Berg Collection

Preface

THE POEM Pope published as *The Dunciad* in 1728 was the core of a work that occupied him in one way or another for at least half his life. He called this satire his "chef d'oeuvre"; he said that no work had cost him more pains—probably both in the labor it exacted and the antagonism it provoked. Its reception at the initial publication on 18 May 1728 reflected the animosity toward Pope that had been building for a decade and a half but also adumbrated the difficulties that lay ahead. According to Richard Savage, "On the Day the Book was first vended, a Crowd of Authors besieg'd the Shop; Entreaties, Advices, Threats of Law, and Battery, nay Cries of Treason were all employ'd, to hinder the coming out of the *Dunciad:* On the other Side, the Booksellers and Hawkers made as great Efforts to procure it."[1]

This *Dunciad* was one of Pope's three major volleys in what Savage said was commonly called "the *War of the Dunces*" from

---

1. *Collection*, vi. Most of Savage's history of *The Dunciad* is reprinted in Johnson's Preface to the Works of Pope (*Lives*, 3:147–49). Johnson says that the account is by Pope himself; Savage's biographer Clarence Tracy disagrees, though he readily acknowledges that Savage provided Pope with anecdotes of Grub Street life (104–10). Robert Carruthers's *Life of Pope* contains a nineteenth-century depiction of the scene at the bookshop (facing p. 264; reprinted in Mumby, facing p. 194). Birkbeck Hill says that Savage's description refers to publication of the 1729 *Dunciad Variorum* (*Lives*, 3:149n), but that edition was first distributed instead by three of Pope's noble friends.

Preface

1727 through 1730.² Pope's first shot had been his *Peri Bathous: or, Martinus Scriblerus His Treatise on the Art of Sinking in Poetry;* it occupied the place originally designated for *The Dunciad* in "The Last Volume" (issued March 1728) of what are now called the "Pope-Swift *Miscellanies.*" A year after this guide to degraded versification, which mustered samples of contemporary writing for its models, Pope issued *The Dunciad Variorum.* Here he extended and made more explicit the satire of the first version of the poem by filling in the numerous initials and blanks and adding extensive notes and other prose apparatus. Noting the counterattacks, one of the assistants on Pope's translation of the *Odyssey* wrote to a fellow collaborator in the early summer of 1729, "The war is carried on against him furiously in pictures and libels."³ Indeed, Joseph Guerinot's *Pamphlet Attacks on Alexander Pope* records forty-four separately published assaults on Pope in those four years.

The text of the first *Dunciad* has been virtually ignored since it was succeeded by the *Variorum.* In two and a half centuries it has appeared in print only a handful of times, usually in corrupt versions, and the standard modern edition conflates it with later varieties. The single attempt to represent the appearance of the 1728 text is likewise inadequate in satisfying the modern interest in the significance of layout and in Pope's fussiness with typographical details; that 1928 type facsimile shares the problem of textual corruption, and it is difficult to find. One purpose of the current volume is to present the text and typography of the earliest edition in a form as close to the original as photofacsimile will allow.

The *Dunciad* reproduced here is a copy of the large-paper

---

2. *Collection,* iv. Another participant in the controversy, Edmund Curll, also spoke of it as a military engagement. In the *Daily Journal* of 12 May 1729 he advertised what, despite his wording, were previously published works now reannounced to take advantage of the attention surrounding the new *Dunciad Variorum:* "This Day is Open'd The Second Campagne of the Dunciad Wars With a New Edition of [eight anti-Pope works]."
3. Elijah Fenton to William Broome, 24 June 1729 (*Corr.* 3:37).

Preface

issue now in the Berg Collection of the New York Public Library. That copy is of special interest and importance because it contains collations that Pope's friend Jonathan Richardson, Jr., made of the 1728 text and a manuscript draft of the poem. The *Dunciad* volume in the Elwin-Courthope edition of Pope's *Works* of 1871–86 cited many of these, but their full scope was not widely known until 1984, when Maynard Mack transcribed them as well as those from a second *Dunciad*, now also in the Berg Collection, in *The Last and Greatest Art: Some Unpublished Poetical Manuscripts of Alexander Pope*. A second goal of the present work, therefore, is to complement the work of Professor Mack. Ordinarily he presented both photographs and transcripts but was kept from doing so here by economic considerations reinforced by the realization that these *Dunciad* materials were already one remove from the hand of Pope. A facsimile is nonetheless useful, for it serves as a way of checking the transcript and of clarifying relations among the annotations Richardson crammed in the margins.

The accompanying essay is designed to elaborate on the implicit emphasis of the facsimile, namely, the development of the poem to its earliest printed forms. To accomplish this third purpose, the essay combines earlier surveys of *The Dunciad*'s progress with the products of new research. The resulting treatment is a series of narrowing circles: the development of *The Dunciad* as a literary work (through its gestation, birth, and—briefly—its subsequent maturation); the physical characteristics of the poetic text and frontispiece in the edition of 1728; some features of the Berg copy of the poem; and the nature of Richardson's annotations. In order to extend the usefulness of the volume as a guide to the composition, production, and reception of the 1728 *Dunciad*, it concludes with a series of appendixes of other relevant material.

This new edition has encountered the problems common to most photofacsimiles. Variations in the ink of the notes do not show up in the photographs; these may point to different stages of annotation, and I have indicated the discernible differences in section 4. I have compared the page proofs of the facsimile against the original *Dunciad;* although that procedure does not guarantee that all readings, especially those of the manuscript notes, are unambiguous, it does confirm that there have been no inadvertent additions or deletions in the course of reproduction. The *Dunciad* is reproduced in its original size. The image on a typical page (9; C1^r) is 105 (115.3) × 73 mm (from the beginning of the lineation to the end of the pagination); that leaf itself measures 209 × 129 (top)/127 mm (bottom).

The edition is "noncritical" in that it reproduces the text of a particular document rather than providing an editorial construction of a text that comes "closer to attaining some desired standard than any of the surviving documentary texts happen to do."[4] The 1728 Berg *Dunciad* is nonetheless representative of copies of its impression; except for its apparently unique broken comma at the end of 3.126, it contains no formes whose readings vary from those in the other twenty examples I have examined (eight of which I have machine-collated). The appendixes provide much of the textual apparatus commonly associated with a critical edition. It has seemed worthwhile to record this information not simply because no such edition appears imminent but more importantly because it constitutes part of the history of this volume's subject, the 1728 *Dunciad*, and places the particular copy presented here in the wider context of its impression and edition.

This volume is the outgrowth of other work on the poem, which has been supported in part by research fellowships from the William Andrews Clark Memorial Library and the Bibliographical Society of America, a National Endowment for the Humanities Summer Stipend, and Summer Grants from the University of Virginia. The present project has been completed during the tenure of a Sesquicentennial Associateship

---

4. Tanselle, 37. This essay offers a convenient summary of editorial approaches and the issues to be considered with each.

Preface

from the University of Virginia and with the special help of my colleagues Martin Battestin, Fredson Bowers, Ralph Cohen, and, in ways that would amuse him, the late Irvin Ehrenpreis; Ruthe Battestin, Nancy Essig, and Kendon Stubbs of the Bibliographical Society of the University of Virginia; Lola Szladits and Richard Newman of the New York Public Library; Kimball Higgs of the Grolier Club; the staff of the University Press of Virginia, and Warren Chappell; John Bidwell, Thomas V. Lange, G. Thomas Tanselle, and Michael Winship; the librarians and other friends in the United States, Canada, England, and Ireland who have provided *Dunciad*s and advice; and Doris, Rebecca, Rachel, and Sarah, who have participated in the quest for *Dunciad*s, provided its motivation, and shared its accomplishment. To all and for all of these I am thankful.

Abbreviations

Works frequently referred to have been identified by the following abbreviations. Full publication data are given in the list of Works Cited.

ART — Maynard Mack, *The Last and Greatest Art* (1984).

COLLECTED — Maynard Mack, *Collected in Himself* (1982).

CORR. — Alexander Pope, *The Correspondence of Alexander Pope*, ed. George Sherburn, 5 vols. (1956).

EC — Alexander Pope, *The Works of Alexander Pope*, ed. Whitwell Elwin and William John Courthope, 10 vols. (1871–86).

FOXON — David Foxon, *English Verse 1701–1750*, 2 vols. (1975).

GRIFFITH — Reginald H. Griffith, *Alexander Pope: A Bibliography*, 1 vol. in 2 parts (1922–27).

GUERINOT — J. V. Guerinot, *Pamphlet Attacks on Alexander Pope 1711–1744* (1969).

LIFE — Maynard Mack, *Alexander Pope: A Life* (1985).

SPENCE — Joseph Spence, *Observations, Anecdotes, and Characters of Books and Men*, ed. James M. Osborn, 2 vols. (1966).

SWIFT CORR. — Jonathan Swift, *The Correspondence of Jonathan Swift*, ed. Harold Williams, 5 vols. (1963).

TE — Alexander Pope, *The Twickenham Edition of the Poems of Alexander Pope*, John Butt, General Editor, 11 vols. in 12 (1939–69).

The History of Pope's
DUNCIAD

1728

I · THE WORK

Gestation

THE ORIGINS OF *The Dunciad* are obscure, but Jonathan Swift's description of Pope's method of composing the poem rings true. In "Dr. Sw—— to Mr. P——e, While he was writing the *Dunciad*," Swift wrote:

> Now Backs of Letters, though design'd
>   For those who more will need 'em,
> Are fill'd with Hints, and interlin'd,
>   Himself can hardly read 'em.
>
> Each Atom by some other struck,
>   All Turns and Motion tries;
> Till in a Lump together stuck,
>   Behold a *Poem* rise![1]

Swift points especially to the piecemeal nature of the process: the lines originate separately on discrete pieces of paper, the passages undergo continual modification, and the sections coalesce only gradually into an integral unit with a common theme. Such is the method implicit in Richardson's own cluttered record of Pope's *Dunciad* drafts; such is also the inference from particular passages within *The Dunciad* itself. Those observations furthermore correspond with the pattern that one of the ablest twentieth-century students of Pope, George Sherburn, detects in the composition of Pope's poems that are more fully documented: "Pope worked by paragraphs or pas-

---

[1]. Swift's poem was first published in the fourth volume (entitled "The Third Volume") of Pope and Swift's *Miscellanies*, 1732 (²72–74).

sages and . . . his great problem was arranging the paragraphs and tying them together tactfully" ("Pope at Work," 55). Sherburn also notes how elements originally part of one work are shifted to another, and how throughout the process Pope employs what he called "The last and greatest Art, the Art to blot."[2]

Four of the earliest fragments that eventually found their way into *The Dunciad* illustrate well the "Turns and Motion" of elemental passages. The first of these survives from an epic poem, *Alcander, Prince of Rhodes*, that Pope variously identified as having written "a little after I was twelve" (*Spence*, Item 37) or "at 15 years old" (*Corr.* 1:467n)—either way, in the opening years of the century. Pope's friend Joseph Spence records his saying that the simile of clocks' weights (1.169–70),[3] as well as a couplet on the circulation of the blood (3.47–48), first appeared in *Alcander* (*Spence*, Item 41). The image next occurs in Pope's poem "To the Author of a Poem call'd *Successio*": "As Clocks run fastest when most Lead is on" (*TE* 6:15). Although that poem was not printed until 1712, Pope said in a note to *Dunciad* 1.177 in his 1735 *Works II* that he wrote the poem "at Fourteen Years old" (i.e., in 1702 or 1703). Though it is possible that Pope misremembered slightly when recalling events of three decades earlier, it is plausible that he would have been most inclined to satirize the author of another poem when it was new and its topicality fresh. That would argue for an early date in accord with Pope's statement, for the poem to which he responds, Elkanah Settle's "Eusebia Triumphans. The Hannover succession to the imperial crown of England, an heroick poem," was first published in 1702.[4]

---

2. Line 281 of "The First Epistle of the Second Book of Horace," quoted from *TE* 4:219.

3. For ease and clarity and unless otherwise specified, all line numbers refer to the 1728 edition reprinted here. I have not attempted to correct the mislineation that occurs at two places in book 2. The citations are approximately the same as from the *A* version of the Twickenham text, but not inevitably so.

4. *Foxon* S253, from which I quote the title. *Foxon* also lists editions or issues in 1704, 1705, 1709, 1711, and 1715.

The Work

About 1704 Pope met the well-known dramatist William Wycherley, whose recent *Miscellany Poems* had met an unfavorable reception. Wycherley appreciated the bright youth and welcomed the help Pope could provide in polishing his verse.[5] In a letter of 20 November 1707 (*Corr.* 1:31–32) Pope discussed modifications of Wycherley's poem "A Panegyrick on Dulness." Among other changes, he spoke of heightening the similitude of the "Clock-Weights." Pope's defensiveness here about introducing new material and a note in his 1729 edition of the second volume of Wycherley's *Works* (see *Corr.* 1:32n) reveal that he had replaced a single line—identical with that which appeared in his own poem "To the Author of . . . *Successio*"—with the four-line version, first printed in Theobald's 1728 edition of Wycherley's *Works*:

> So Clocks to Lead their nimble Motions owe,
> The Springs above urg'd by the Weight below;
> The pond'rous Ballance keeps its Poize the same,
> Actuates, maintains, and rules the moving Frame. (1:2.14)

Some critics have contended that the solitary line was originally Wycherley's, but in the 1729 note Pope suggests that he was the author, having proposed it to Wycherley in a letter of 3 April 1705 (no such letter is now known).

The histories of the other two images, the flying lead and biased bowl, are similar to that of the clock weights. The lead simile had first appeared in Pope's "*Successio*" poem, written as early as 1702, according to his 1735 note, and then published in 1712: "So, forc'd from Engines, Lead it self can fly, / And pondrous Slugs move nimbly thro' the Sky" (*TE* 6:16). The example of the flattened ball used in lawn bowling was another that Pope introduced into Wycherley's "Dulness" poem in 1707 and Theobald printed in 1728:

> The Poize of Dulness to the heavy Skull,
> Is like the Leaden Byass to the Bowl,

---

5. Maynard Mack discusses Pope's involvement with Wycherley and Wycherley's works in *Life*, 94–100.

> Which, as more pond'rous, makes its Aim more true,
> And guides it surer to the Mark in view;
> The more it seems to go about, to come
> The nearer to its End, or Purpose, home. (1:2.14)

In a letter of 25 June 1711 Pope explained to his friend John Caryll the reasoning behind his use of such illustrations: "I've often known that when all the precepts in the world would not reclaim a sinner, some very sad example has done the business" (*Corr.* 1:121). The same insight appeared in verse, in lines that most likely are Pope's: "So when the noblest Precepts can't prevail / To mend us, sad Examples never fail." The couplet is from Wycherley's "To a Doctor of Physick," a poem which Pope revised, probably about the time of the letter, and which also appeared in the 1728 *Works* (1:2.69).

The separate lives of these four passages converged when Theobald invoked Dulness in the 1728 *Dunciad*. Pope first sharpened the six-line account of the bowl into two couplets (1.137–40):

> Oh thou! of business the directing soul,
> To human heads like byass to the bowl,
> Which as more pond'rous makes their aim more true,
> Obliquely wadling to the mark in view.

A few lines later, the other three passages congealed—the sad-examples couplet significantly reworked, the flying-lead lines slightly revised, and the clock-weight image reduced from four lines to two (1.165–70):

> So written precepts may successless prove,
> But sad examples never fail to move.
> As forc'd from wind-guns, lead itself can fly,
> And pond'rous slugs cut swiftly thro' the sky;
> As clocks to weight their nimble motion owe,
> The wheels above urg'd by the load below.

The works in which these passages appeared are interesting as well for their indication of Pope's early interest in topics and themes that would later find expression in *The Dunciad*. *Alcander*, which like both Settle's "Successio" and the 1728 *Dunciad* itself was labeled "An Heroic Poem," was set in the time of the Trojan War,⁶ the same period that lies behind *The Dunciad's* most frequently invoked classical parallel, Virgil's *Aeneid*. In *The Dunciad* Pope is preoccupied for a thousand lines with the same Dulness that Wycherley treats in miniature in his "Panegyrick" to that quality.⁷ Pope's poem to Settle, his earliest published satire, is the richest of all in its connections with *The Dunciad*. Most significant is its parallel theme: he mocks Settle's dutiful paean to the Hanoverian succession by transforming the political sequence to a poetical one in which Settle becomes the heir of dull writers. To do so, he also employs elements which later appear in *The Dunciad*, including scatology and the name "Codrus" for Settle.⁸

Settle indeed figures prominently in the next recoverable stage of *The Dunciad's* composition, around 1720. According to the poem itself, the action takes place on the Lord Mayor's Day that inaugurated the term of Sir George Thorold. As Pope pointed out in a note at 1.83 in the 1729 *Dunciad Variorum*, Thorold held that office for most of 1720, his yearlong

---

6. This according to the senior Richardson's transcript of Pope's dictation, reprinted in Sherburn's "New Anecdotes," 346.

7. Citing examples from Dryden on, James Sutherland notes that "almost every writer in this age, even the dullest, seems to have been acutely conscious of dullness in the air" (*TE* 5:xxxix). Isobel M. Grundy discusses verses on the topic by Lady Mary Wortley Montagu and her cousin Henry Fielding that appeared shortly after *The Dunciad*. Both, she observes, "represent an attempt to turn Pope's weapons against himself" (213).

8. One other couplet deserves mention as an example of an early passage successively modified. Lines 42–43 in a 1709 manuscript of *An Essay on Criticism* read, "Tho' such with reason Men of Sense abhor, / Fool against Fool is barb'rous *Civil War*" (Schmitz, 32–33). They next appear in 1717, as lines 4 and 5 of the Prologue to *Three Hours after Marriage* ("Blockheads with Reason Men of Sense abhor; / But Fool 'gainst Fool, is barb'rous Civil War" [*TE* 6:178]), and then, further revised, in Richardson's *Dunciad* collations and as *Dunciad* 3.145–46. The play is generally considered a collaboration by Gay, Arbuthnot, and Pope; the Twickenham editor cites the reappearance of these verses in *The Dunciad* as evidence that Pope in particular wrote the Prologue.

mayoralty actually beginning on 29 October 1719.⁹ Pope presents the aging Settle (b. 1648), the last of London's official city poets, as performing his function of versifying for the occasion (1.78) in what proves to be his swan song. Settle's subsequent death (1.175 and note) provides the occasion for the poem as the goddess Dulness selects and installs his spiritual successor.

These references, as well as Settle's underworld prophecy in book 3, led Sherburn to speculate that Pope wrote a satire on dullness in poets near the time of the specific Lord Mayor's Day that marked Thorold's induction. He hypothesized that this poem on the model of Dryden's *MacFlecknoe* may have originated as a satire on the choice of a city poet, in burlesque of the recent selection of a *national* laureate in December 1718 when Laurence Eusden succeeded Nicholas Rowe (*Selections*, 450–51). Robert W. Rogers further observes that John Dennis, born in 1657, would at this time have been the age he speaks of at 2.261 (10–11). Together these factors suggest that this progenitor of the full *Dunciad* might have been written around 1720.

One problem with that chronology is that Settle did not die until 12 February 1724. But because Settle's income had steadily dwindled until in about 1718 his friends had secured room for him in the Charterhouse hospital (according to the *DNB*), Pope may have observed that Settle's powers had already waned irretrievably and that debate about his successor was timely. Indeed, Settle's poor financial condition would make Pope's appellation for him, "Codrus" (2.124), all the more appropriate, for the ancient Roman poet of that name was proverbial for his poverty (as Pope explains in a note to 2.136 in the 1729 *Variorum*).

On the other hand, Pope's confident assertion of Settle's death may suggest that part of this version was not written until at least 1724. His reworded description of Settle's passing in the *Variorum* (1.88n) may reflect his own attempt to recon-

---

9. *The Post-Boy*, 29–31 Oct. 1719. Since the calendar shift in 1752, the official date of the celebration has been 9 November.

cile the conflict in dates: Pope's new word *demise* could refer in its older, legal sense to the devolution of Settle's sovereignty in the realm of dullness rather than specifically to his death. Be that as it may, the existence of part of the poem already in the early 1720s would help explain Pope's contention in the 1728 Preface that "this work was the labour of full *six* years of his life."

It may have been such a version from the early 1720s that Jonathan Swift saved from destruction. According to a note in the 1729 *Variorum* (attached there to a reprint of the 1728 Preface), "the first sketch of this poem was snatch'd from the fire by Dr. *Swift*, who persuaded his friend to proceed in it, and to him it was therefore Inscribed." The note implies that the rescue occurred as the men were sorting materials for their volumes of *Miscellanies*, the first two of which appeared in the spring of 1727. If so, Swift intervened during the spring or summer of 1726, his first visit to London in twelve years, during which he spent most of his time at Pope's villa in Twickenham.

The manuscript that Swift rescued may have been the one that contained a passage from Spenser. As Spence was reading the *Faerie Queene* in Pope's study in 1744, Pope told him that he had "at first designed for my motto to the *Dunciad*" the stanza from the poem (1.1.23) in which the Red Cross Knight, fighting the offspring of Error, is likened to a gentle shepherd molested by "A cloud of combrous gnattes." Spence, who had known Pope since 1726, recalls that he himself "had seen it writ down many years ago before, in his original Mss Copy of the Dunciad" (Item 420). There is no record of the motto in the transcriptions Richardson made of the manuscripts that, as I will propose, appear to define the poem's contours from 1726 to 1728. This "original Mss Copy" therefore may well have been from the first half of the decade and the one that Swift rescued.

Even before Swift's 1726 arrival the friends had discussed material that was to become part of the poem. On 15 October

1725 Pope had sent a passage which, he said, formed "a very good conclusion of one of my Satyrs, where having endeavour'd to correct the Taste of the town in wit and Criticisme, I end thus"—with verses on Ambrose Philips. The concluding line ("When Ambrose Philips was preferr'd for wit!") eventually appeared near the end of *The Dunciad* itself (at 3.274). At the same time Pope, with his characteristic suspicion of being intercepted in the post, declined to reveal fully "what designes I have in my head . . . till I see you here, face to face" (*Corr.* 2:333). Swift's response was in terms also commensurate with there being a work like *The Dunciad* in view: "Take care the bad poets do not outwit you, as they have served the good ones in every Age, whom they have provoked to transmit their Names to posterity[.] Maevius is as well known as Virgil, and Gildon will be as well known as you if his name gets into your Verses; . . . the difference between good and bad Fame is a perfect Trifle" (26 Nov. 1725; *Corr.* 2:343–44).

Swift's early connection with the poem led both him and Pope to indicate that Swift was somehow responsible for it. The title page of the first edition announced that the poem had earlier been published in Dublin—with the almost inevitable implication that it might have been written by that prominent satirist in Dublin, Swift. On 12 October 1728 Pope contended in a letter to Thomas Sheridan that "my Friend the Dean . . . is properly the Author of the Dunciad" (*Corr.* 2:523). The same day he wrote Swift about "how much that poem is yours . . . since certainly without you it had never been" (*Corr.* 2:522). Swift himself asserts that "I had reason to put Mr. *Pope* on writing the Poem, called the *Dunciad*" (July–2 Aug. 1729; *Swift Corr.* 4:53). Jonathan Richardson, Sr., confirms that "in 1726 & 7 Dr Swift coming to England passed the Summer with him at Twickenham, and before he went, perswaded him to write the Dunciad" (quoted in Sherburn, "New Anecdotes," 347).

The verdict of the editor of Pope's correspondence, Sherburn, on these declarations that Swift was the fundamental

The Work

author is succinct: "absurd" (*Corr.* 2:522n). According to him, Pope was "somewhat too eager to involve Swift with himself as an ally against the Dunces." Sherburn is quite right in sensing Pope's anxiety about bearing the brunt of the Dunces' retaliation, but he overlooks ways in which these hints at a collaboration might nonetheless be accurate, and he does not acknowledge the playfulness implicit in some of them.

Swift does seem to have contributed directly to later editions of the poem, and he may have done so for the first version as well. Sherburn in fact maintains (without explanation), "It is a safe guess that his brilliant idea was the making of Lewis Theobald hero" (*Selections*, 451). Writing shortly after the initial publication, Swift advised Pope to annotate his parodies and, contrary to his earlier warning about immortalizing the victims, to fill his "Asterisks" with "some real names of real Dunces" (16 July 1728; *Corr.* 2:505). He later claimed credit when Pope revised; he had encouraged Pope, he writes, "to hale those Scoundrels out of their Obscurity by telling their Names at length, their Works, their Adventures, sometimes their Lodgings, and their Lineage; not with A——'s and B——'s according to the old Way, which would be unknown in a few Years" (July–2 Aug. 1732; *Swift Corr.* 4:53). Swift may have responded to Pope's request that he provide notes for those later editions (28 June 1728; *Corr.* 2:503). As a founder of the Scriblerus Club with Pope and others in about 1713, he might also have had a role in germinating the plan of *The Dunciad*, which follows the Scriblerians' agenda of exposing contemporary folly and dullness.

The claims of Swift's responsibility, moreover, can be interpreted in ways consistent with Pope as the genuine writer of the poem. If Swift actually rescued a draft from the fire, he could legitimately be considered the one to whom the work owed its existence. He could also be viewed as its "author"—not as "writer," but as one who offered suggestions and encouragement and thereby caused the poem to be. Some of the ascriptions to Swift, moreover, need to be seen in the playfulness of their context. First, although the Dublin imprint might suggest that the work was Swift's, it also would further confuse the dunces and leave their judgment uncertain. Second, both Pope and Swift joked about the way in which Swift was responsible. In the poem "Dr. *Sw*—— to Mr. *P*——*e*, While he was writing the *Dunciad*," Swift identifies himself as the "*causa sine quâ non*" of the poem. He explains:

> Thus, *Pope*, in vain you boast your Wit;
> For, had our deaf Divine
> Been for your Conversation fit,
> You had not writ a Line

—just as a sexton "justly half the Merit claim'd [for the accomplishment of a famous preacher] / Because he *rang the Bell.*" Alluding to the onset of Swift's deafness during his 1727 visit to London,[10] Pope makes a similar point in his letter to Sheridan: *The Dunciad* "had never been writ but at his Request, and for his Deafness: For had he been able to converse with me, do you think I had amus'd my Time so ill?" (*Corr.* 2:523). Swift seems crucially responsible, then, for encouraging Pope in his writing and perhaps even for offering specific suggestions, but some of the assignment of credit is simply the result of a private joke.

It was not only Pope's friends but also his enemies who nudged *The Dunciad* into shape. For nearly his entire adult life Pope had been the object of bitter criticism: from the time in 1711 when John Dennis had called the misshapen young man "venomous . . . stupid and . . . impotent as a hunch-back'd Toad" (*Reflections*, 26), Guerinot records attacks in fifty-seven pamphlets up to the publication of *The Dunciad*. Pope's own list in the 1729 *Variorum* adds hostile newspaper accounts as well, a record that no modern scholar has yet had the energy to develop in full. As Guerinot points out, the assaults were comprehensive. Pope's enemies attacked his deformity, reli-

---

10. Swift himself gives the best account of his ill health in a letter to Thomas Sheridan on 12 August 1727 (*Swift Corr.* 3:228–29).

gion, income, and satiric impulse; they charged that his work displayed indecency, blasphemy, stupidity, and ingratitude.

In 1725 Pope responded to Swift's warning about immortalizing scribblers by agreeing that the best response was to ignore and outshine them, but in the same letter he showed that his frustration was only barely restrained: "It would vexe one more to be knockt o' the Head by a Pisspot, than by a Thunderbolt" (14 Dec.; *Corr.* 2:350). Indeed, the vexation increased as the dunces devised new provocations. In July 1726, for instance, Pope's old nemesis Edmund Curll embarrassed him by publishing his youthful and sometimes bawdy letters to Henry Cromwell—"unbuttoned effusions," as Mack calls them.[11]

But the publication of Theobald's humiliating *Shakespeare Restored* a few days before Swift's arrival in March 1726 was probably the most important of the incitements inching the text toward its first published form. Though Pope had been irritated by Theobald throughout the previous decade,[12] at this point he seems to have elevated him to the central role in *The Dunciad*. Theobald was the ideal centerpiece; he perfectly embodied the functions of farce-writing dramatist, occasional poet, periodical journalist, and pedantic editor and critic that Pope in his developing satire was identifying as generators of cultural degradation. Theobald's appropriateness thus did not depend on any personal connection with Pope, though his book on Shakespeare's text attacked Pope with a bluntness that made it especially satisfying for Pope to welcome him to the poem. Theobald's title explains that he produced his work in direct response to Pope's 1725 edition of the plays: *Shakespeare Restored: Or, A Specimen of the Many Errors, as Well Committed, as Unamended, by Mr. Pope In his Late Edition of this Poet. Designed Not only to correct the said Edition, but to restore the True Reading of*

---

11. *Life*, 655; Pope describes these letters and the circumstances of their publication in the *Variorum* note at 2.66.
12. Mack surveys the relationship of Theobald and Pope and summarizes Theobald's Shakespeare criticism in *Life*, 426–33.

Shakespeare in all the Editions ever yet publish'd. His dutiful recounting of Pope's improper emendations, his promise of an even more thorough examination, and his implication that Pope had intentionally misstated the extent of his collations embarrassed and enraged the editor who had labored diligently on his six-volume edition and who indeed had contributed usefully to the development of Shakespearean textual criticism.

The increased attention that Pope gave the poem during Swift's 1726 visit continued with Swift's final stay in London the following year, when Pope's references to the work became more frequent and specific. In sketching the contents of the *Miscellanies* volumes, Pope and Swift seem to have assigned this "Dulness" poem to the end of "The Last Volume," the one devoted to poetry. Throughout 1727 Pope spoke as if a publishable form of the poem were now within sight. On 30 June he wrote the *Miscellanies* publisher, Benjamin Motte, that "the Poem, which I will have to end the Volume . . . will make 3 sheets at least," or forty-eight octavo pages (*Corr.* 2:438); when published, the poem and its preliminary leaves took up six and one-half half sheets. But he also suggested to Motte that it might be advantageous to have the poem "published singly first" and that he would not be finished with it until winter. Thus, by the time he announced to Oxford that "our Miscellany of Poems will be published next October" (25 Aug. 1727; *Corr.* 2:444), thereby implying that the shape of the volume was fairly well set, he seems already to have determined to withhold *The Dunciad*. December found him still scrambling to find material to fill the resulting gap in the *Miscellanies* volume; on the twenty-sixty and twenty-eighth, for instance, he wrote Oxford about including a poem of Matthew Prior's.

After Swift left for Dublin on 18 September 1727, Pope continued work on *The Dunciad*. On 22 October he wrote Swift about a revised form, though, as earlier, he feared interception of the correspondence and declined with regret to send an actual copy (*Corr.* 2:455–56). He expressed the same reticence

The Work

the following January in a letter that included the poem's opening proposition, "Books and the Man I sing" (*Corr.* 2:467–70). In these instances, however, he did include versions of the developing dedication of the poem to Swift, which both Bolingbroke (*Corr.* 2:472) and Swift (*Corr.* 2:498) expected would appear in the poem. But after writing Swift, Pope had further thoughts; before the poem was even published he was planning a revised edition, the *Variorum*, for which he would withhold those verses (see *Corr.* 2:498). They did indeed appear in 1729, and then in a form revised still more. Whatever the full explanation of the postponement, one effect was to leave open the possibility that the poem was by Swift himself.

Despite Pope's care in concealing his hand, the advent of the poem was becoming widely anticipated. On 5 February 1728 Edward Young wrote in remarkable detail to Thomas Tickell: "Mr Pope is finishing a Burlesque Heroik on Writers, & ye modern diversions of ye Town, it alludes to Virgil & Homer thro[ugh]out. The 5th book of Virgil is burlesqud into games, in wh Booksellers run for Authors, & Piss for Authoresses &c; as is likewise part of ye 6th by a Vision of Heroes in Dullness &c: tis near done, & what is done is very correct" (60–61). The name of the poem also became known, and one of the most striking changes as it neared publication was in the title. In January 1728 Pope still referred to his "Poem of Dulness," and he joked that bound copies would be labeled accordingly: "*Pope's Dulness*" (*Corr.* 2:468). As late as February, Bolingbroke wrote Swift that "*Dulness* grows and flourishes" (*Corr.* 2:472). But upon reflection Pope realized that the humorous ambiguity of the title would be at too much expense to himself. Indeed, the writer of "A Letter against Mr. P. at large" (John Dennis, according to Pope in the *Variorum*) reported in the *Daily Journal* of 11 May that Pope was currently writing the *Progress of Dulness* and pointed out that those who had read "*Windsor Forest*, . . . the *Temple of Fame*, . . . the *What d' ye call it*, . . . [and] the *Profound*" were already familiar with that account. Only months before publication, therefore, Pope made an important but secret announcement to Swift: "my *Dulness*," he wrote, "for the future you are to call by a more pompous name, the *Dunceiad*" (23 Mar. 1728; *Corr.* 2:480).

Meanwhile, the delay caused by refining the poem was testing Pope's forbearance. According to Pope, the great felicity of his life, second only to cultivating friendships with worthy contemporaries, was "to get rid of fools and scoundrels"; echoing a theme from the *Faerie Queene* stanza, he wrote Swift that "this Poem will rid me of those insects" (23 Mar. 1728; *Corr.* 2:481). As the wait increased, so did the attacks, particularly in response to the publication of Pope's *Peri Bathous* in "The Last Volume" of the *Miscellanies* on 8 March 1728. In the letter "The Publisher to the Reader" that prefaced *The Dunciad* itself in May, Pope described the outcry: "Every week for these two Months past, the town has been persecuted with Pamphlets, Advertisements, Letters, and weekly Essays, not only against the Wit and Writings, but against the Character and Person, of Mr. *Pope*" (iii–iv; italics reversed). Meanwhile Pope's friends were becoming impatient. "Why does not Mr Pope publish his dullness," asked Swift of John Gay; "the rogues he mawles will dy of themselves in peace, and So will his friends, and So there will be neither punishment nor reward" (26 Feb. 1728; *Corr.* 2:475).

Birth

THE DUNCES did not go gently into their night. Pope finally published *The Dunciad* on 18 May 1728, and the responses were those adumbrated by the earlier correspondence and gossip. Swift's opinion was typical of Pope's friends: "After twenty times reading the whole, I never in my opinion saw so much good satire, or more good sense, in so many lines" (16 July 1728; *Corr.* 2:504). The subjects of the poem had a different view: "The whole Piece is so notoriously full of Pride, Insolence, Beastliness, Malice, Prophaneness, Conceits,

The Work

Absurdities, and Extravagance, that 'tis almost impossible to form a regular Notion of it," wrote James Ralph in the Dedication to his *Sawney* (iii). According to Pope's and Guerinot's lists, more newspaper and pamphlet attacks appeared in the year immediately following publication than in any comparable period of Pope's life. Gay reported to Swift that "Mr. Pope is in a state of Persecution for the Dunciad" (6 July 1728; *Swift Corr.* 3:292), and the earl of Oxford confirmed the situation with a pun that indicated his own attitude: "Mr. Pope stands by himself Athanasius Contra Mundum; there is never a Newspaper comes out but he is favored with a letter; a poem and Epigram even to a Distich from the newmorous Herd of Dunces and Blockheads that are in and about London and the Suburbs there of" (27 July 1728; *Corr.* 2:507).

This outcry came despite Pope's efforts to conceal his authorship. The title page carried no name, and the imprint stated that the edition was merely a reprint of one that had earlier appeared in Dublin—implicitly, by an Irish author.[13] The only book trade member identified, Ann Dodd, probably had no direct responsibility for the publication, and in any event her profession as a "mercury," or distributor or seller of newspapers and pamphlets, would make her connection with a particular author too vague to be meaningful. David Foxon suggests that Pope himself had paid the printing costs and recovered his outlay—and the profits—from the pamphlet-sellers; given the wording of Savage's description of the dunces besieging a single shop, he furthermore suspects that Dodd's premises in particular had sold the 1728 poem.[14]

---

13. Commentators at least as late as Allibone believed that the poem had first appeared in Ireland (*Critical Dictionary*, 1625). According to *Griffith*, for instance, "Dilke says (*Papers of a Critic*, I, 323) that [John Wilson] Croker long maintained, and was never quite satisfied to the contrary, that the Dunciad, as professed, was first published in Dublin" (2:283). The implausibility of such judgments may have spurred the interest that arose in *The Dunciad*'s bibliography midway through the nineteenth century.

14. *Pope and the Early Eighteenth-Century Book-Trade*, sections I and III, where Foxon also provides the most thorough examination of Dodd's function in the trade. In his Introduction to Fielding's *Covent-Garden*

Pope's contemporaries appear to have known of his involvement in the marketing of the satire; a writer in the *Daily Journal* of 9 September 1728 observed that "as is said, . . . he makes a little Profit by the *retailing* of it."

The person who entered the book in the records of the Stationers' Company and deposited the required nine copies there on 30 May, the poem's printer, James Bettenham, did so in his own name, without indicating Pope's authorship. The introductory letter "The Publisher to the Reader" acknowledged that some readers would identify Pope as the author but suggested that similarities to Pope's writing were deliberately misleading; the writer also observed that Pope was widely associated with the Greek poet Homer but that the *Dunciad* author seemed to have a greater admiration for the Roman Virgil. Finally, the last page of the duodecimo issue announced the forthcoming publication of a work by the title the world associated with Pope's incubating satire: "The Progress of Dulness." Because he had declined to send even his friends a copy of the later phases of his widely known project, the dunces would not have had a sure knowledge of the details of the poem. Pope then used the notice that a poem by the title of the anticipated one was forthcoming to deflect certainty about his authorship in still another way.

Some of Pope's reticence in claiming credit for *The Dunciad* may have stemmed from his plan to publish a fuller edition, in which he could contend that this first one (which would serve him by provoking the dunces to make responses that he could incorporate in the second) was published without his authority. But he also seems to have anticipated reprisals and sought to minimize their impact. The expected storm of verbal oppo-

---

Journal, Bertrand A. Goldgar draws on the help of J. Michael Treadwell in sorting out the various Dodds of the early eighteenth-century book world. He identifies the "A[nn]" of Pope's imprint as the widow of a printer named Nathaniel Dodd and the mother of another Ann (b. 1716), who inherited the shop when the mother died in April 1739. These Dodds were apparently unconnected with another Nathaniel Dodd, "whose business was once managed by Thomas Gent" (xix).

sition contained threats of physical violence as well. A pamphlet published on 1 June, *A Popp upon Pope*, purported to give an account of an actual attack. The author, whom Pope believed to be his estranged friend Lady Mary Wortley Montagu, reported how one evening near the Thames two men ambushed Pope and beat his "naked Posteriors" so hard that he "voided large quantities of Blood"—which was yellow because of the gall in it.[15] Likely resenting the attributed humiliation and fearing the incendiary effect of such an account, Pope publicly denied its accuracy in an advertisement in the *Daily Post* on 14 June.

Though Jonathan Richardson, Jr., later reported that "no one was ever more tender and sore to raillery than *Pope*" (*Richardsoniana*, 311), Pope's half sister Magdalen Rackett described him as wary but unintimidated by the events of 1728. "My brother does not seem to know what fear is," she told Spence; on the solitary walks he much enjoyed, "he would take Bounce a great, faithful Danish dog . . . with him, and for some time carried pistols in his pocket" (Item 265). When Spence himself warned Pope about walking alone, "he said that 'the people I mentioned were low and vile enough, perhaps, to be capable of such designs, but that he should not go a step out of his way for them, for let the very worst that I could imagine happen, he thought it better to die than to live in fear of such rascals'" (Item 266). On 17 June Pope was able to thank an acquaintance "for his kind Concern about my person, which hath hitherto remaind as Unhurt (I thank God) as my Temper, by these Scoundrels" (*Corr.* 2:502).

The special interest of contemporary readers was in the satire as a *poème à clef*; their response has helped sustain the unquenchable charge that Pope was more interested in vilifying individuals than the follies they symbolize. Swift's response upon first seeing the published *Dunciad* is representative: "I have long observ'd that twenty miles from London no body

---

15. *Guerinot* (114–16) summarizes the pamphlet and quotes it extensively; see also *TE* 5:xxii–xxiii.

understands hints, initial letters, or town-facts and passages; and in a few years not even those who live in London. . . . it will be a great disadvantage to the poem, that the persons and facts will not be understood, till an explanation comes out, and a very full one. . . . You must have your Asterisks fill'd up with some real names of real Dunces" (16 July 1728; *Corr.* 2:504–5). The earl of Oxford made a similar request (27 May 1728; *Corr.* 2:496), but both he and Swift had been anticipated by an even greater authority. As Pope wrote back to Oxford, "I have received a Command for the same thing from the Highest & most Powerful Person in this Kingdom" (17 June 1728; *Corr:* 2.502)—the royal person to whom Robert Walpole would present a copy of the *Dunciad Variorum* the following year.

Ten days after *The Dunciad* appeared, Edmund Curll, whose own prominence in the poem made him an interested observer, published a twenty-four-page *Compleat Key to the Dunciad* in which he offered to explain "all the Passages, Pieces, and Persons Libelled, in that scurrilous, obscene, and impious Satire" (*Evening-Post*, 1–4 June). Within a month Pope issued two new printings of the poem—and Curll responded to each with a new edition of his annotations. Contemporary accounts cite two other keys as well. One, attributed to Curll's writer Thomas Cooke (in *Mist's Journal* of 8 June), may be the anonymous four-page *Key* that is extant in about half a dozen copies. Several times, including in the final edition of his own *Key*, Curll also mentions a third: he says the bookseller Lewis has one in manuscript. Presumably he refers to William Lewis, Pope's Roman Catholic schoolmate and the publisher of the *Essay on Criticism*. Not one to miss an opportunity, Curll says that copies of that *Key* are available to those who contribute a "Peter-Penny" toward the purchase of "a *Wooden Crucifix* and a set of *Horn-Beads*" (3d ed., vi).

There were also responses to the work that did not constitute such independent keys but which served many of the same functions. A 1728 edition published in Dublin (*Foxon* P770) filled up many of Pope's blanks with names, and con-

The Work

temporary readers did the same by hand in their own copies, just as they had done for satires like Dryden's *Absalom and Achitophel* and Garth's *Dispensary*. When Pope published the embellished poem as *The Dunciad Variorum* the following spring, he incorporated such elucidations into the work itself: he filled most of the blanks, and he added explanatory notes—often from the previous keys. Curll was not yet finished either: without flinching at, or perhaps without noticing, the full implications of parallelism implicit in his title, he immediately produced *The Curliad*, which commented at length on Pope's use of the Curlian keys in the *Variorum* and which contained "A farther Key to the New Characters."

These keys reveal much about the immediate response to the poem. The volume—and volumes—of replies first of all confirms what is no surprise, the contemporary interest in the work. But the replies also indicate the geographical range of interest and the effect of distance from London in promoting befuddlement about the poem. Although the Dublin edition completes many of the initials, it also leaves a great many unfilled. And when it does venture a name, the result often is wildly inaccurate. Scotland may have had a key as well, at least if David Foxon's surmise is correct that the "Gold chains" edition of the poem (P769) was printed in Edinburgh. Whenever I have found the anonymous four-page key, it occurs with this unauthorized edition, which has the reading "Gold chains" for "Glad chains" in line 1.76.

The kinds of comments the keys make also reveal much about the audience response. Curll and the others are concerned chiefly with details, not themes; with characters, not broader actions. While interesting in itself, this feature is doubly important because as widely distributed works the keys were able in turn to influence the response of other readers. Indeed, the impulse to read the work as a *poème à clef* continues to the present; the standard Twickenham Edition even quotes Curll for identifications that Pope and his commentator Scriblerus fail to make.

It is not completely accurate, however, to say that the keys

Pope's DUNCIAD of 1728

do not offer interpretations. They occasionally do, again with the double impact of both revealing and encouraging contemporary reaction. The most provocative explanation of Curll's is that Pope is satirizing the court; he makes the point three separate times (in notes to 1.5–6, 1.116, and 3.251). A *Dunciad* now in the British Library has a related notation, one that is legible only, perhaps appropriately, under black light. Toward the end of the first book, where the text describes "a Monster of a Fowl! / Something betwixt a H—— [probably "Heidegger"] and Owl," a contemporary reader has filled the blank with "Hanover." A second theme Curll develops is that of Pope as a nasty man. He is one who burlesques Holy Scripture, who attacks those who have not offended him, and who takes credit for the writing of others, barbarously pummels those already down, and inhabits a body best fit for a masquerade.

Finally, the keys reveal the uncertainty—and perhaps the excitement—surrounding the early interpretation of the poem. Some of the puzzlement is reflected in the discrepancies in identification from one key to another. But it is also apparent in the different editions of Curll's own key. The references to the court, for instance, do not appear until the second edition; it is as if Curll and his circle only gradually came to realize what they could make of the poem. In many other places, too, the texts show Curll's thought developing: from Dennis to Shadwell (3.16), for instance; from Higgons to Howard (1.240); or from Roper to Ridpath (2.129). And at one point Curll suggests his special perplexity as he shifts not once but twice: from Herbert to H——y, and then finally to Hoadley (2.325).

One result of Pope's progressive identification of actual dunces, strengthened by the corroboration that other commentators provided, was exactly what Swift had warned against. Henry Fielding later observed that Pope "may indeed be said to have raked many out of the Kennels to Immortality, which, tho' in somewhat a stinking Condition, is to an ambitious Mind preferable to utter Obscurity and Oblivion" (*Cov-*

ent-Garden Journal, no. 59 [15 Aug. 1752], 321). When Johnson praised the concluding lines of the poem, Boswell elicited a similar comment from him: "It was worth while being a dunce then. Ah, Sir, hadst *thou* lived in those days! It is not worth while being a dunce now, when there are no wits" (16 Oct. 1769; *Life*, 412).

Maturation

THOUGH *The Dunciad* had now achieved the form represented in the facsimile that accompanies this essay, Pope had by no means finished with the poem. Three major revisions followed, in thirty-three separate editions and about sixty impressions and issues by the time of the first posthumous collections of his *Works* in 1751. As with the 1728 version, germs of the later texts can be detected long before their publication. The dedicatory lines to Swift, which finally appeared in the 1729 *Variorum*, are one such instance. Another readily available example lies in Jonathan Richardson's transcriptions of an early *Dunciad* draft (see, for instance, pages 16 and 25 in the facsimile); already before the 1728 edition Pope was noting classical parallels of the kind he would cite in the notes of the *Variorum*.

The Dunciad Variorum was published in April 1729, less than a year after *The Dunciad in Three Books*. It is of special interest in a consideration of the 1728 *Dunciad*, for its alterations—and the resulting contrast with the earlier form—were the most dramatic of any of the redactions of the work. Though the number of lines of verse remained about the same, the length of the overall work quadrupled. Pope made three major changes: he added long prefatory and appended sections of prose; he provided what in another context Johnson would call "illustrative," "judicial," and "emendatory" notes, to the extent that these often exceeded the amount of poetic text on a page;

and in the poem he filled most of the blanks and the abbreviated names.

Pope's use of blanks or initials and dashes in 1728 fit the common notion that this vagueness reduced susceptibility to charges of libel, but the practice served several other purposes as well. Refusing to give full names accorded with Pope's wish to minimize the significance of individual authors in the work; as he says in the "Publisher to the Reader" section, "the poem was not made for these Authors, but these Authors for the Poem," adding that new ones could be clapped in as they rose from day to day. In the "Advertisement" of 1729 Pope also pointed out the value of cultivating secrecy: readers are tantalized by it, and they feel all the better when they think that they finally understand the mysteries. Meanwhile, the blanks created a market for an edition that would literally spell-out the targets; the introductory "Publisher to the Reader" even called explicitly for such a version (v). The incomplete names also encouraged the reader's participation; to make full sense of a line, the reader would be tempted to write part of it. The result was that any libel was arguably the fault of the reader, not the author; any onus associated with satire that was too specific would rest on the reader, for the author had spoken only in a general way. The author had the further advantage that the names, and hence the satire, would tend to be timely. Although the initials that did appear helped to guide the reader's contribution, the assistance was not constrictive: the reader could insert the most relevant example, and the satire was only strengthened by multiple solutions if, for instance, "Selkirk" and "Shylock" fit "S——k" equally well.

Most of these advantages were lost when Pope filled out the names, but others accrued. Though the satire became more determinate, and possibly weaker, as some potential targets were ruled out, the identifications offered better evidence for the poem's general assertions. They also provided readers with the exhilaration of acquiring inside information. The newly added notes offered the same benefits, though the mere pres-

The Work

ence of such commentary implied that the meaning could be fixed. Yet while reader involvement waned in some ways, it grew in others: the work became what our age might call "interactive," in that the text became subject to modification by readers' comments, many of which were recorded in the notes (and, when they thus became part of the text, literally affected the shape of the work).

The author of a nineteenth-century key unexpectedly provides insight into another contribution of these annotations. In the preface of her *Key to Uncle Tom's Cabin* (1853), Harriet Beecher Stowe explained that her base work "had a purpose entirely transcending the artistic one, and accordingly encounters at the hands of the public, demands not usually made on fictitious works. It is *treated* as a reality,—sifted, tried, and tested, as a reality; and therefore as a reality it may be proper that it should be defended" (ix). What Stowe seems to be describing is what the *Dunciad*'s keys and many of its footnotes—especially those incorporating identifications from the keys—do for their host work: they translate fiction into fact; they connect the world in the text with the human world outside of the book. Pope's initials and blanks do not inevitably refer to living people, but the filled blanks and the notes make them do so. By the same token, these features connect the general truths about human life found in the poem with the world of human existence outside of the work, whether other literary sources and parallels or real people and events.

The 1729 version was reprinted many times throughout the fourteen-year term of its copyright, usually under the supervision—and with the revision—of Pope himself. Some of the editions included extensive changes. The second octavo edition of 1729, for instance, added new epigrams to footnotes, and the form which appeared in Pope's quarto and folio *Works II* in 1735 showed significant reworkings of the text (many of which were not incorporated into later editions). In 1742 Pope published what first stood as an independent poem, *The New Dunciad*, but which the following year was printed as book 4 in the final major redaction of the work, *The Dunciad in Four Books*. Though the original three-book form underwent substantial revision throughout, the most obvious internal change was the substitution of the poet laureate Colley Cibber for the earlier hero Lewis Theobald, whose biological existence also ended shortly thereafter. (In one of history's interesting synchronicities, Theobald's life covered the same years as Pope's: 1688–1744.) This four-book version came as part of what subsequently has been known as the "deathbed edition" of Pope's major writings; under the aegis of an editorial theory that implicitly has held the latest form of a work to be the most important, it is the one that editors beginning with Warburton (who added new, possibly Popeian, footnotes) have almost invariably reprinted.

The three-book version of 1728, in contrast, has been reprinted only a few times in the past 260 years. The first editor to include it as a separate work was Joseph Warton, who in his 1797 collection (reprinted 1822) did so for literary reasons: "THAT the Reader may see at one view, the nature, conduct, and coherence of this Poem, how perfect it was in three books, and how much it suffered, and was disfigured, by a fourth book, and by a new hero, the Dunciad is here added, as it stood in the quarto edition, 1728" (5:335). But Warton's execution of the task he set for himself was odd: there had of course been no quarto publication until the *Variorum* of 1729, and it is essentially this that he reprinted—except that he used the text from the second 1736 octavo edition of Pope's *Works*. He sheared the poem of its explanatory notes, but he kept the *Variorum*'s Arguments to each book, and he made no effort to eliminate the readings that had entered between 1729 and 1736. In 1803 J. J. Tourneisen of Basel reprinted Warton's note and three-book text in his edition, as did W. L. Bowles in 1806 and a consortium of London booksellers in their eight-volume set of 1812.

In the twentieth century, James Sutherland, the editor of the standard Twickenham Edition of the poem (first published in 1943), also recognized the value of the early form of the text and consequently printed both A and B versions of *The Dunciad:* the three-book and four-book forms. But for the A text he too used the *Variorum,* specifically the edition of 1729. The reader can recover the approximate form of the 1728 poem by stripping away the footnotes and inserting the earlier textual readings that Sutherland identifies. That historical record, however, is incomplete: it contains most but not all of the variations in wording in the poetic text, and it ignores completely the differences there in spelling, capitalization, punctuation, and italics (what W. W. Greg called "accidentals"). It also reprints the "Publisher to the Reader" letter from the 1729 edition without comparing the readings of 1728.

Several editors, however, have reproduced a 1728 text with reasonable accuracy. The first to do so was W. J. Courthope in volume 4 of the long-standard Elwin-Courthope edition of 1882; an American edition published by Thomas Y. Crowell in 1896, in other respects a revision of the 1869 Globe edition by A. W. Ward, reprinted that text (and Courthope's notes) verbatim, except that it dropped the reproduction of the frontispiece. Basing his work on the 1728 octavo, Courthope modified about 120 accidentals and also silently emended two line misnumberings (the original 2.130 and 2.205) and two obviously incorrect words ("Spirits" at 2.159 and "attempted" at 2.234 of the 1728 text). In 1928 Oxford University Press included a type facsimile of the 1728 *Dunciad* in its series of literary reprints; its concern with imitating the appearance of the original resulted in the most accurate reproduction of the poem yet published.

Only one edition in print today contains the 1728 version: Herbert Davis's edition of Pope's *Poetical Works* issued as part of the Oxford Standard Author Series in 1966. In the poetic text Davis makes fewer than five-dozen changes in accidentals, chiefly in the course of modifying Pope's quotation marks to fit modern, British practice. He does not reprint the 1728 "Publisher to the Reader" but instead cites the version he prints with *The Dunciad in Four Books*, which he takes from the 1743 edition. The practical result is that this edition misrepresents the 1728 address to the reader by adding elaborate footnotes, altering accidentals in over one hundred instances in these six pages, and changing the wording at about eighteen spots. Most significant among these modifications are the deletion of five lines at one point and the elimination of the final two paragraphs of the letter.

    The two decades in which Pope guided the poem to its public debut were thus mirrored by the years in which he revised subsequent editions. In the following two centuries only a few editors have acknowledged the significance of the editio princeps. But just as Pope's own changes disguised the character of the 1728 text, so ironically have many of these attempts because of their misrepresentation of the object of their concern.

II · THE EDITION

DESPITE THE INTENSE INTEREST that surrounded *The Dunciad* from the start and continues, among other places, in modern auction rooms, there has been little certainty about which form of *The Dunciad* was actually the first. And where there has been certainty, there usually has been less than conclusive evidence.

Serious attempts to clarify the publishing history of the poem began in the 1850s, and bibliographers have now identified three typesettings, or true "editions," of the 1728 *Dunciad in Three Books*. The initial impetus came from William Thoms, editor of *Notes and Queries*, who solicited the help of his readers in preparing a checklist of varieties. Thoms enjoyed recounting an episode that proved the need for an accurate record of these relationships, though in part he made his point unwittingly. He had once argued with Lord Macaulay in the Library of the House of Lords over Pope's apparent scorn of the greatest English writer of an earlier age. Thoms understood "furious *D——n*" (1.94) to refer to Dryden; Macaulay took from the shelf a copy of what Thoms called a "later edition" to show that the reading actually was "furious *D——s*" and could not possibly allude to the former laureate. Thoms restrained himself with smugness: "He had all the time in his pocket a copy of one of the first editions of the *Dunciad* of 1728 with the name 'Dryden'" (Solly, 301).

Though Thoms indeed had an early edition, it was an Irish reprint (*Foxon* P770) in which the printer had filled most of the name blanks—without authority, and often inaccurately (see the listing in Appendix 2). In the *Variorum* Pope noted the "Dryden" alteration, as he did the change of "Glad chains" to "Gold chains" (1.76) in still another unauthorized republication. In a tradition that assigned any anonymously reprinted text to the most famous of contemporary literary pirates, Edmund Curll, Pope's bibliographer R. H. Griffith surmised that the latter edition probably issued from his shop. More recently, David Foxon has suggested that instead it is one of many such reprints of Pope's poems produced in Edinburgh (see *Foxon* P769).

Both these editions derived from the one James Bettenham printed for Pope in London. Pope would have wanted this explosive work handled by a printer whose discretion he could trust, and he probably had known Bettenham for some time. Bettenham had been an apprentice to William Bowyer, who had printed many of Pope's earlier works, and he had married Bowyer's stepdaughter. He himself had printed three volumes of the duodecimo edition of Pope's *Iliad* in 1720–21. His religious politics, moreover, were in the direction that the Roman Catholic Pope would appreciate, for a 1724 census classified him as a non-juror;[16] indeed, in 1726 he printed the sermons of Pope's exiled friend Bishop Francis Atterbury. That he produced *The Dunciad* is suggested by its printer's ornaments, which also occur in other works with his name in the imprint in the 1720s,[17] and is confirmed by the testimony of one of his apprentices, Daniel Prince, who told how he was the one "trusted to go to the Author with the proofs in great secresy" (Nichols, 3:705).

---

16. Negus, in Nichols, 1:302.
17. For instance: Robert South's *Sermons* in six volumes (1727), or the first two editions of Anthony Sparrow's *A Rational, or Practical exposition of the Book of Common Prayer* (1722). I am grateful to John Chalmers, Librarian of the Harry Ransom Humanities Research Center at the University of Texas in Austin, for enabling me to identify these publications through his ornament file.

The Edition

Once scholarly opinion had successfully identified the original edition, the relationships of the various issues and impressions remained to be sorted. Although Pope later denounced the 1728 *Dunciad* as "imperfect" and "surreptitious," he took his characteristic care in its production, not only reading proof but also issuing the book in both ordinary- and fine-paper formats. Within three weeks of the first publication on 18 May, so-called second and third editions also appeared (on 24 May and 8 June; *Foxon* P766–67). In actuality, each of these was merely a reimpression from standing type, with roughly one gathering in each reset. The same is true of a second "Third Edition" (P768), which must have followed shortly but whose publication date is uncertain.

Determining which of the first two issues had priority has occasioned some of the nastiest squabbling in Pope studies since the original War of the Dunces. The books were printed on the same varieties of paper, but the duodecimo had twelve pages on each side of a sheet and the other only eight. The sheets were printed by the work-and-turn method. The type for all the pages of the gathering, instead of for only half of them, was on the press at one time; the finished sheet, printed on both sides, would (when cut in half) yield two copies of half a normal gathering instead of one copy of a full one. In collational formulas, the structure of these books would be described as follows: $12°$: A-E^6 F^2 and $8°$: a^4 b^2 B-G^4 H^2, with an equal number of pages in each version. Because each page imposed in the octavo format occupied a larger percentage of the original sheet, it would have wider margins; the octavo therefore served as a deluxe "large-paper" issue. (The copyright law required that the copies deposited with the Stationers' Company be on the best paper, and it was in fact the octavo issue that Bettenham placed there.) Scholars had long recognized that the octavo was not advertised separately until 30 May, but the wiser among them also realized that such information meant nothing about the printing order of the two, even if the duodecimo had been distributed first.

Although it was chiefly human curiosity that demanded resolution of the question of priority, there were also practical reasons. As an auction reporter for the *Times Literary Supplement* observed apropos *The Dunciad*, "In an atmosphere like the present, . . . the slightest doubt of the complete and unquestionable priority of edition is usually enough to make a book unsaleable at almost any price" ("Notes on Sales," 32), and hundreds of early twentieth-century pounds depended on the outcome. There were, moreover, fifteen differences between the two texts (listed in Appendix 1), including the first word, where the duodecimo read "Books" but the octavo had "Book." In 1906 Thomas Lounsbury contended in *The Text of Shakespeare* that "Book" referred to Theobald's *Shakespeare Restored* and that the text thereby supported the dominant nineteenth-century view of Pope's malignity in fingering Theobald out of personal pique. Lounsbury sneered that "modern bibliography has obligingly come to Pope's aid" in contending that the singular form of the word "is nothing but an error of the press which passed unheeded and uncorrected" by the "author, type-setter, proof-reader, and reviser" (290).

R. H. Griffith published his early reflections on the priority of the issues in 1915 and developed his argument more thoroughly in the first part of *Alexander Pope: A Bibliography* in 1922. His discussion is punctuated with remarks such as "But I am not sure" and "What I think happened," but he cautiously decided that the duodecimo was the first printed. The eminent British book dealer, collector, and bibliographer T. J. Wise took issue with Griffith the following year in the fourth volume of *The Ashley Library* catalogue. The contrast of his tone was striking: he proposed to provide "a final record of the complete series of editions of *The Dunciad* of 1728" and asked, "Does Professor Griffith seriously mean what he appears to assert?" The "curious opinion held by Professor Griffith—but by no other person capable of judging upon the matter—" that the duodecimo came first was, according to Wise, "laborious and involved; [it] is based upon no supporting facts, and consists mainly of his own suggestions and suppositions." Not surprisingly, Wise gave precedence to the octavo. Griffith returned to the matter in an appendix to the second part of his bibliography in 1927. He remained tentative about his own conclusions, but his language hardened, and he was certain of the merits of Wise's argument: "Of all the points, then, set forth in the pages of the Ashley *Catalogue* not a single one affords any support whatever to either of the two propositions, that there was a small octavo London edition of the Dunciad in 1728 [Wise, developing a suggestion of Thoms, had argued for a *third* issue of the first Bettenham *Dunciad*], or that the octavo edition preceded the duodecimo edition" (583).

The debate continued for another decade but then lay dormant for twenty years while various writers called for the question to be resolved once and for all. In 1931 Wise reiterated his points in *A Pope Library*, a slightly revised version of the Pope section of *The Ashley Catalogue*. Griffith had the last word in this phase of the controversy: the year after Wise died, he drew on some points raised in a 1931 article by W. K. Chandler to state with a definitiveness he had earlier found unacceptable that "the *princeps* of the *Dunciad* was the duodecimo" ("The Dunciad Duodecimo," 582). In 1958 Foxon applied his considerable abilities to the question. He too noted that his insights did not yet solve all of the problems, but he sided with Griffith in favoring the priority of the duodecimo. Especially significant were aspects of his methodology: he was the first both to use the mechanical assistance of the Hinman Collator to compare the texts and to acknowledge that priority for one part of the work did not entail priority for all parts ("Two Cruces").

Most of the discussion had rested on the interpretation of the minor textual differences between the two forms. When one reading was clearly better than the other, two chief explanations were possible: either the faulty text had been corrected for the second printing, or the better readings had been corrupted as the text was reimposed. The problem with *The Dun-*

ciad was that the same facts could support either pattern; further complicating the matter was that some passages were "better" in the duodecimo, others in the octavo. Realizing this, the contestants drew upon other forms of evidence: that the dimensions of the type page argued the type had been set for one of the formats rather than the other; that if two of three forms (including subsequent "editions") agreed, those two were chronologically adjacent; that a "good" state of the text would remain once it had been incorporated; and that the *Progress of Dulness* advertisement present in the duodecimo but not the octavo entailed unmistakable priority for one of the issues.[18] But none of these generalizations proved unambiguous when applied to *The Dunciad*, and the verdict remained inconclusive.

A close examination of the two issues reveals textual differences that even the scrutiny of the earlier investigators did not detect. Unfortunately, these changes too are indefinite in their significance. What proves more helpful is the pattern of the running titles at the top of each page. In order to avoid the work of resetting the headings each time, the compositors would reuse these units from one sheet to the next, modifying only the page or book numbers as appropriate. With the precision that the Hinman Collator allows, individual running titles can be traced throughout the different issues and impres-

---

18. Wise proposed a complicated scenario in which the printer of *The Dunciad* surreptitiously placed an advertisement for an actual *Progress of Dulness* (which appeared on 15 June) on the final blank of Pope's duodecimo issue and subsequently removed it in the face of Pope's rage. Griffith, taking his cue from Lounsbury, argued that not only this advertisement in *The Dunciad* but also the ones tacked onto notices for the poem in newspapers constituted a diversion planned by Pope. Griffith seems to me correct. Pope's role in publicizing his works in newspapers has never been probed, but in at least one other instance he drew up the wording, specified the papers, the number of repetitions, and the typography, and requested that the notice appear "at the head of the more vulgar advertisements at least rankd before Eloped wives, if not before Lost Spaniels & Strayd Geldings" (Pope to Samuel Buckley, 20 Jan. 1725; *Corr.* 2:285). His control over the printing of the 1728 *Dunciad* and the coupling of the announcements for the poem and *Progress* piece suggest that he was also responsible in this instance.

The Edition

sions of the book. Their pattern seems to point to certain unexpected but inescapable conclusions about the order of production: the pressmen first printed gatherings B and C (pp. 1–24, or roughly the first half of the poem) of the duodecimo, then the same pages—but now gatherings B, C, and D—of the octavo, followed by D and E (pp. 25–48) of the duodecimo and then the comparable E, F, and G of the octavo. Thus, each of these sections (and by analogy, the introductory prose and the final four pages as well) was first printed in duodecimo, then the type was reimposed on the bed of the press for production in octavo. That means, however, that not only the duodecimo but also the octavo forms of the first half of the poem were completed before the second half of either was begun. Griffith's assessment of priority had been essentially correct, but in a way that he had not anticipated. These same running titles were also reused for the remaining three Bettenham impressions in duodecimo. Their pattern, coupled with the evidence of resettings of some pages of the text, enables us to determine the order of printing for sections of those subsequent impressions as well: gatherings E, D, C, and B of the "second edition"; gatherings B, C, D, and E of the first "third edition," and gatherings D and E, C, and B of the second "third edition."[19]

Foxon has also noted that the layout of the 1728 text may have special significance. Briefly stated, his suggestion is that the format imitated two famous series of classical works: one from the seventeenth century by the Dutch firm Elzevier, and, from the early eighteenth century, one edited by Michael Maittaire and issued in London by the publisher Jacob Tonson and printer John Watts. Foxon observes that Tonson innovatively extended this design to serious English works as well, including, for instance, his 1711 duodecimo edition of *Paradise Lost*. One of the first of Pope's works to be published in a small

---

19. I explain these patterns in greater detail in "The Printing of Pope's *Dunciad*, 1728."

format, the third edition of the *Essay on Criticism* printed by Watts in 1713, was similarly designed (possibly by Pope), and it was this poem's typography that Pope copied in the *Dunciad* of 1728. The first *Dunciad* therefore gave the impression of being an English classic, an implication that would be made another way in 1729 when Pope presented the poem in the "variorum" form usually reserved for ancient works (Lyell Lectures, sections I.iv and III.ii).

One other physical feature of prominence in the book is the engraved frontispiece, which introduces the poem by bringing together some of its important verbal images and which reinforces the satire by making them visible. The central object is an altar constructed of books by authors ridiculed in the pages that follow: Colley Cibber, the duchess of Newcastle, John Dennis, John Ogilby, Lewis Theobald, and Sir Richard Blackmore. On the altar sits an owl—not merely the bird of Dulness in the poem (as at 1.25 and 1.234) but also "a symbol of benighted wisdom and ill omen" in "classical, Biblical, native, and natural" tradition.[20] At the foot of the engraving, the imprint mirrors the message of the title page that the work was first published in Dublin and now reprinted in London for A. Dodd.

By stressing the foolishness associated with owls, Pope may also be taking a swipe at Edmund Curll. On 26 July 1726 Curll had published a two-volume set of *Miscellanea* (*Griffith* 177–80). The first part only deepened the old rift between the men, for it contained embarrassing youthful letters from Pope to Henry Cromwell. In *The Dunciad* Pope identifies the purveyor of this correspondence as "C[ur]l's Corinna"; he elaborates on the circumstances of publication in a note in the *Variorum* (*TE* A.2.66). The possible connection with the frontispiece occurs

---

20. McKenzie, 26. McKenzie traces the transformation from the owl's early connection with Athena and wisdom. Mengel also considers the 1728 frontispiece (162–65). Entries 1793 and 1794 in the British Museum *Catalogue of Prints and Drawings* describe the authors contributing to the altar and identify the lines in which they appear in the poem.

The Edition

in the second volume of *Miscellanea*. In *Laus Ululae. The Praise of Owls*, a separately paginated tract with its own title page, Curll aligns himself with owls and their associations. The frontispiece features a perched owl in its upper center, as in *The Dunciad* (though in *Laus Ululae* the other chief features are a flock of birds circling the owl and, below, a man pointing to it). In the text, the author (presumably Curll or his hack) dredges classical learning and lore not only to broach such questions as What came first: the owl or the egg? (29) but more importantly to show that owls are properly considered signs of good rather than ill. The very need to offer such a thesis reflects the popular presumption against it; by possibly alluding to this work, Pope may have been using Curll's voluntary defense of the symbol of dullness in the same way that he would later quote the dunces' own words against themselves.

The designer and the engraver of the frontispiece are not recorded, though Pope's known limning abilities have made him an attractive candidate for the first of those roles. Pope had taken painting and drawing lessons in 1713–14 from Charles Jervas, eventual King's Painter to George I and George II. Pope's own sketch for the frontispiece of a posthumous edition of the *Essay on Man* still exists; as another indication of his interests, an inventory taken at his death located seventeen of his drawings in his garret.[21] On the other hand, one of Pope's good friends was the artist William Kent, who had prepared dozens of designs for the *Odyssey* of 1725–26 and who would contribute others to the *Essay on Man* in 1734 and to the *Dunciad* that appeared in Pope's *Works* in 1735; he conceivably could have drawn the 1728 frontispiece, in which case it might have been engraved by the person who executed Kent's earlier and later designs for Pope, Paul Fourdrinier.

---

21. A sketch long believed to be Pope's, now in the Lewis Walpole Library in Farmington, Conn., is reproduced as the frontispiece to the Twickenham *Essay on Man*. John Riely has recently identified Pope's apparent original in the Hofer Collection at the Houghton Library, Harvard. The inventory was reprinted by "F. G." in *N&Q*, 6th ser. 5 (13 May 1882): 363–65.

Among other candidates for designer among Pope's artistic acquaintances one should not overlook the Richardsons themselves—the father a well-known portrait painter and the son a follower in that profession.

David Foxon's reminder in his Lyell Lectures of Pope's detailed concern with the physical appearance of his works adds additional plausibility to Pope's involvement with the illustrations. But care must be taken not to let these pieces of circumstantial information develop into certainties. Given the evidence we have, the statement of one commentator that "we must assume that he is responsible for all the *Dunciad* prints" (Mengel, 161) is valid only when it is severely qualified, as indeed that critic goes on to do. It does seem likely that Pope would have influenced the nature of the frontispiece in a book whose publication he undertook without the customary guidance of the book trade. But more than that we can not yet say.

The subsequent fortunes of the 1728 engraving are similar to those of the verbal text. The plate was immediately pirated with the rest of the work for the "Gold chains" edition; the care and expense that its reproduction represent give the lie to the popular impression that such unauthorized editions were always produced with maximum haste and at minimum cost. Like the poetry, the engraving reappeared in the subsequent Bettenham issues, though without the analogous alterations made in the text. That situation changed in 1729, when the plate was used in the first octavo edition (following the original quarto) of the *Dunciad Variorum*. The banner was changed to reflect the poem's new title, the Dodd imprint removed because the book was now "Printed for Lawton Gilliver," and some worn lines of the image retouched.

But soon—after about a fourth of the copies had been printed, according to the surviving evidence, or at the time when the plate began to appear in combination with that of the vignette of the book-laden ass taken from the quarto title page—Pope (we assume) made changes akin to those taking place in the text. The successive incarnations of the poem illustrated the principle enunciated in the 1728 preface that authors' names "were clapp'd in as they rose" and "chang'd from day to day," and the engraving did the same. Whereas the top book of the altar had initially been labeled "P. & K. Arthur," it now read "Gildon & Woolston. ag.st Xt." The name of the author of the Arthur poems, Blackmore, replaced that of Newcastle near the bottom of the pile. One more change lay in store: in the 1735 octavo (reissued in 1736) Pope changed "Dennis's Works" in the pedestal to "Oldmix: Hist: of Stuarts." (The relationship of these alterations appears graphically in Appendix 3.) The authors had indeed become interchangeable; what was important about them was not what they had to say but rather features they would consider incidental, accidental, and ultimately demeaning: how well they served Pope's purposes by illustrating dullness or serving as the inert elements in a physical monument to that quality.

III · THE COPY

THE *Dunciad* reproduced in the following pages is one of two in which Jonathan Richardson, Jr., transcribed for Pope the readings of manuscript drafts of the poem. These copies of the 1728 and 1736 octavos, in their original blue-gray wrappers, are both in the Berg Collection; each is uncut and affords the largest possible space in the margins for annotations. In addition, the stitching at the spine of the 1728 edition has been removed to permit maximum use of the gutter as well. The cover of the 1728 octavo carries the notation "N[o.] 3" in an early hand; the 1736 copy has "N 1" in the same script and ink. What appears to be the offset marking "N 2" occurs on the back of the 1728 volume; it may have been the identification on another 1728 copy that belonged to Richardson, the one that is now at the Huntington Library (RB 106517), for the title pages of all three books bear the signature "Jonat. Richardson jun. / Queen's Sq." On the titles of the Berg copies Richardson—or, quite possibly, Pope—has indicated that the 1728 edition is "corrected" from the "First Broglio MS." and the 1736 one "alterd from the Second MS."

These books and various manuscripts that Pope gave Richardson (see section 4) apparently remained in Richardson's possession until his death in 1771 when, according to Mack, they "made their way, without ever going on public sale, into the collection of Charles Chauncy" (*Collected*, 325). The migration of these documents since the eighteenth century is part of the larger and as yet uncharted course of Pope's poetical manuscripts in general. But at least some parts of the history of these *Dunciad*s can be reconstructed. Because the copies are easily confused, it is well to record what is known about each of them.[22]

The common manuscript date "1777" on the titles of the three copies seems to indicate that in that year they were part of a single collection, probably that of Dr. Charles Chauncy, F.R.S. (1706 or 1709–1777) or his brother and heir Nathaniel. According to Seymour de Ricci, Chauncy "had formed a valuable collection of books, nearly all in choice condition and in handsome bindings. He was one of the earliest bibliophiles to pay attention to literary manuscripts or presentation copies" (57). In particular he was one to pay scholarly regard to his acquisitions, as shown by his notes in the volume now in the Berg Collection that contained among other Pope material a copy of the *Essay on Man* and the manuscript of the *First Satire of the Second Book of Horace*. He may also have been responsible for the note on the title of the Huntington *Dunciad:* "N. All here added or changd is from a Copy of Mr Popes of this same Edition."

But then parts of the trail become obscure. The 1728 Berg, or "First Broglio," copy remained in the family throughout most of the nineteenth century, probably having first passed (as did the *Essay on Man* volume, according to annotations in it) to brother Nathaniel and then to Nathaniel's nephew Charles Snell Chauncy. During the Chauncy custodianship the Elwin-Courthope editors consulted it; Courthope thanks Elwin for

---

22. Griffith may have been one of those misled by the lack of a clear record. He says: "There is . . . a copy of the octavo edition of 1728 in the possession of Mr. Henry E. Huntington, of Los Angeles, California, upon the margins of which Jonathan Richardson the Younger copied variant readings from what he called the 'Broglio Ms.' These readings are reproduced in E-C, IV, 271, ff., notes" (149). I suspect that Griffith assumed the octavo with the "Broglio" markings and the other one that Richardson owned, with a few notes also based on Pope's, were the same. I have not found evidence that Huntington ever owned the "Broglio" copy, including any record of its dispersal in catalogues of Huntington duplicate sales from 1916 through 1925. It is not the kind of book that one imagines Huntington parting with.

"his liberality in allowing me to use his transcript of the Chauncy MS. [probably to be construed as plural], which throws so much light on the meaning of Pope's satires" (*EC* 3:x). In a note to his reprint of the 1728 *Dunciad* Courthope again identifies the source of the manuscript variants, though in slightly different terms: "Jonathan Richardson corrected the first edition of the 'Dunciad' from what he calls 'the first Broglio MS.' His corrections have been transcribed by Mr. Elwin, and are here preserved" (4:271). With this comment in mind, Sutherland in the Twickenham Edition speaks consistently of "the EC MS." (in notes on pp. 99, 142, and 184, for instance), a rendering that has led some readers to think that a full manuscript still existed until a century ago. Undoubtedly Elwin transcribed Richardson's notes from the current Berg copy; what is intriguing about Sutherland's ambiguous reference to these annotations is that in 1943, the date of his first edition, the whereabouts of the book was not known even to preeminent Pope scholars.[23]

Before its appearance in the Berg Collection, the volume was last in public view at an auction of Christie, Manson and Woods on 30 July 1889. The sale, generally referred to by the name of the chief consignor, General W. Nassau Lees, featured seven lots of the most significant Pope manuscripts now known, all from the library of Charles Chauncy. Before the holographs of such treasures as *An Essay on Man* and *An Essay on Criticism* came this *Dunciad*. It sold for £16, apparently to the dealer Francis Harvey.[24] Its location for at least the next thirty years is unknown. As Dr. Szladits points out in her Foreword, it is likely that Owen D. Young obtained it in the 1920s; what is certain is that it came to its present home in New York in 1941.

---

23. Not that availability would have mattered. *EC* reprinted only some of the manuscript readings, and *TE* sifted them even further. That the *TE Dunciad* records any notations at all is nonetheless remarkable, for the edition was guided by an editorial approach that "excluded manuscript readings on policy" (Butt, 25).

24. According to a marked catalogue at the Grolier Club.

Pope's DUNCIAD of 1728

The early histories of the other two Richardson-Chauncy volumes are more mysterious, though at least one has since led the most visible existence of all. The first modern record of each is in the catalogue of the 1888 Pope Commemoration at Twickenham. The 1736 edition, described as "Pope's own copy" (Item 102), was lent by Richard Tangye, and the other 1728 copy (Item 9) by the Pope bibliographer Lt. Col. Francis Grant. How these left the Chauncy family is unclear, though they may have been dispersed in the Leigh and Sotheby sale of Charles and Nathaniel's libraries on 15 April and 3 May 1790 (Munby and Coral, 89), following Nathaniel's death. After 1888 the 1736 copy disappeared until it too surfaced at the New York Public Library, again as part of the collection of Owen D. Young.

Grant's copy, on the other hand, has attracted periodic surges of attention. After being sold to the London dealer B. F. Stevens at the Sotheby auction of Grant's collection on 8 May 1900, it apparently went on the market again later that year. Perhaps at that time it came to Robert Hoe, for it appeared in the 1905 catalogue of his library and fetched a record amount at its sale by the Anderson Auction Company on 17 January 1912. The price—$1,800—was not only the highest amount known to have been paid for any *Dunciad* but also marked the largest bid at the auction session; accordingly, it formed the subject of headlines in at least five New York papers. The bidding began at a parodic one dollar; ultimately George D. Smith outbid Dr. A. S. W. Rosenbach and, indeed, ended up with thirteen of the fourteen *Dunciad*s in the sale. The newspaper accounts traced the fortunes of the copy over the previous dozen years: the *Sun*, for instance, reported that it had sold at the Grant sale for $325, then again that year for $250. (The *Daily Tribune* reported the first price as £75, in contrast to the marked catalogue at the Grolier Club, which lists it as £45.)[25] Records of the Huntington Library confirm

---

25. Photocopies of accounts from the *New York Times, New York Herald, New York Daily Tribune, Sun*, and *World* are bound at the Grolier Club in a thick volume of clippings about the series of Hoe sales.

that its founder acquired the book at the Hoe sale. According to Charles F. Heartman's biographical account of Smith, Huntington had sat at his agent Smith's side, nudging him when he wished to bid (8–9).

One characteristic permeating the history of these books is that they have been highly prized whenever they have surfaced. Only in the past few decades, however, have the three of them been publicly available at the same time.

IV · THE ANNOTATIONS

THE JONATHAN RICHARDSON who transcribed Pope's *Dunciad* manuscripts was the son of the artist of the same name who often painted, drew, or etched Pope's portrait.[26] The Richardsons' friendship with Pope extended from at least the second decade of the century and seems to have been strengthened by the interest in literary and visual art the three shared. Father and son not only wrote verse and books of art history but also in 1734/5 published their collaboration *Explanatory Notes and Remarks on Milton's Paradise Lost*, which was partly in response to Richard Bentley's edition of Milton's poem in 1732 and which Pope helped them prepare. Pope apparently appreciated the younger Richardson's patience with detail and asked him to collate and record variations in his own works. In the anecdotal collection *Richardsoniana* (1776), Richardson recounted both a cause of that request and one result that is of special interest for the history of Pope's manuscripts:

> As for his *Essay on Man*, as I was witness to the whole conduct of it in writing, and actually have his original MSS. for it, from the first scratches of the four books, to the several finished copies, (of his own neat and elegant writing these last) all which, with the MS. of his *Essay on Criticism*, and several of his other

26. Wimsatt provides a thorough account of the Richardsons' relationship with Pope (137–222).

> works, he gave me himself, for the pains I took in collating the whole with the printed editions, at his request, on my having proposed to him the "making an edition of his works in the manner of *Boileau*'s." (264)

In a letter to the senior Richardson, Pope alluded to the collator's modus operandi: "I have a Particular Book for your Son of all my Works together, with large Margins [probably the quarto *Works II* of 1735], knowing how good an use he makes of them in all his books; & remembring how much a worse writer, far, than Milton, has been mark'd, collated, & studied by him" (17 June [1737?]; *Corr.* 4:78). If the volume was indeed *Works II*, it was probably the one now in the Huntington Library; like the present edition of *The Dunciad*, that copy shows that Richardson did make good use of the margins, for he has there inserted his collations of a manuscript of the "Epistle to Burlington," for instance.

It is not clear when Richardson transcribed the *Dunciad* variants, though several factors suggest the mid or late 1730s. The earliest Richardson collations to reach print appeared at the end of the 1735 *Works II*, where a "Variations" section registered readings from different editions of the *Essay on Man* and several Epistles. Though the date of Pope's letter announcing the gift book to Richardson is uncertain, Sherburn's estimate of it as from the second half of the decade fits with the period of Richardson's known activity (if the book was indeed *Works II* the letter might more plausibly be dated 1735). Because Richardson used a copy of a 1736 *Dunciad* in which to set down the Second Broglio readings, 1736 is the earliest he could have done so. But because the transcription of the First Broglio sometimes refers explicitly to passages recorded in that volume (as on pages viii and 46), it too must have been made not earlier than 1736.

It is more difficult to determine the date of the First Broglio manuscript itself or its relative position in the stages of the poem's composition. The corrections and recorrections

The Annotations

throughout the draft emphasize, of course, that parts of it were composed at different times, but the references to Theobald in the opening and closing lines of book 1 suggest that at least a substantial portion was established after Theobald had been introduced as hero—probably in 1726, as suggested earlier. In the other chronological direction, this version was certainly prepared before the first publication in 1728. That point seems obvious but it needs stating, for the fundamentally similar text of the Second Broglio has often been assumed to *follow* the 1728 edition. Though Pope would still adjust nearly every paragraph before printing the poem, it is present here in the relatively complete form of the 1728 printing; Pope's later assertions that the work was written in 1727 or 1726, the years of Swift's visits, could be considered accurate if he is seen as referring to this draft.[27]

It seems unlikely, however, that the First Broglio was used as printer's copy for the 1728 edition. Judging from the complicated nature of Richardson's transcriptions, the draft was too convoluted to be used effectively as such, and the differences are too extensive to make that possibility seem likely. It may be that the situation for the 1728 edition was like that which Dennis contended applied for the 1729 *Variorum*, that "twenty times the Rhapsodist alter'd every thing that he gave the Printer" (*Remarks*, 8), and it could be that Pope made such modifications on the proofs that Daniel Prince carried between Pope and Bettenham. But there is also a second important reason why I believe *The Dunciad in Three Books* was not set from this draft: there appears to have been at least one other major version between the First Broglio and the 1728 edition, namely, the Second Broglio, the manuscript whose readings Richardson recorded in the 1736 volume.

Critics have been moving toward that judgment, but they have left the matter unresolved. Robert W. Rogers surmised

---

27. The British Museum *Catalogue of Prints and Drawings* points out that a date of 1726 "accords better with the subjects of the satire" than does 1727 (2:653n).

that both Broglio manuscripts "must have been early ones" and offered what he defensively called the "extravagant hypothesis" that even the part of the second manuscript that was later to reappear in book 4 came from around the time of the 1728 edition. Miriam Leranbaum built on his insight to argue that the book 4 material, identified in the Second Broglio as for "Canto 2d," makes it likely that the manuscripts were "written in close conjunction with one another, and preceded the first published edition of the poem," though she did not consider other evidence that might make that argument conclusive. Maynard Mack's statements usually seem to suggest that the Second Broglio came between the 1728 and 1729 versions, although his consistently careful wording allows the possibility that it also preceded the 1728. He observes that the 1736 octavo contains the readings "which Richardson has inserted . . . from the 'Second MS.'—that is to say, presumably, from a sheaf of *Dunciad* papers accumulated while the text of the 1729 *Dunciad* (or even, possibly, the 1728 *Dunciad?*) was in preparation." Although the scholarly verdict thus seems to be leaning toward the hypothesis that both manuscripts preceded the first edition, James McLaverty's observation without demurral that Mack identified "a skeleton plan for *Dunciad* IV already present in the manuscript for the *Variorum* of 1729" appears to imply that the outline and the second manuscript as a whole came after 1728.[28]

Richardson's—or Pope's—note on the 1736 title page ("This Book is alterd from the Second MS; as ye 1st Ed. is from the First MS.") may suggest that the Second Broglio formed the basis for Pope's revisions in the *Variorum*, but it could just as easily be taken literally—that Richardson happened to enter the Second Broglio readings into the recently issued 1736 text that was readily accessible. Conventional wisdom indeed seems to acknowledge that implicitly, for it never seems to have held that the Second Broglio was used for the 1736 pub-

---

28. Rogers, Appendix B, "The Missing *Dunciad* Manuscripts," in *Major Satires*, 120, 122; Leranbaum, 147; Mack, *Collected*, 339–40; McLaverty, 89.

The Annotations

lication, only for the *Variorum* in general. To argue that Pope used the Second Broglio for 1736 in particular would require the implausible hypothesis that the poem developed from the 1728 edition through the 1729 quarto, the first and second octavo editions of 1729, the quarto and folio versions of *Works II* in 1735, and the octavo of 1735; that Pope then recast the poem as the Second Broglio in a form that closely resembled the First Broglio; and that he subsequently modified the Second Broglio to produce a text that returned almost exactly to the most recent one in the series of published editions. At the very least, however, the Second Broglio would have had to precede the 1735 rather than the 1736 octavo, for the 1736 was merely a reissue of the sheets of the 1735 with a new title page and one cancel leaf.

After reconstructing the texts of both manuscripts and comparing them with the 1728 and 1729 editions, I have come to think that not only the First but also the Second Broglio predated the 1728 publication. This, of course, is what the logic of conserving effort would entail; it would make little sense for Pope to recopy the thousand or so lines of the poem once he had a printed version (of 1728) that he could more easily modify. But the most persuasive confirmation is that provided by the readings of the second manuscript, which usually represent an intermediate state between the First Broglio and the 1728 text.

Although a selection of examples cannot convey the force of the cumulative evidence, they can illustrate the pattern. In its various incarnations, what occurs as line 3 in 1728 reads:

MS 1: I sing; say great ones (You these works inspire)
MS 2: Say great *Patricians*! (You these Works inspire!
1728: Say great *Patricians*! (since yourselves inspire
1729: Say great Patricians! (since your selves inspire

Pope alters the first half of the original line for the second manuscript, and changes the second half for the initial printed form. The *Variorum* retains the readings of the previous year, except that in accord with the typographic simplification found in this edition the italic *Patricians!* converts to roman. The division of "yourselves" into two words meanwhile brings it to the form that was to remain in editions throughout Pope's lifetime.

Similar development occurs in the ninth line of book 2, though now the situation is complicated by progressive development within each of the manuscripts:

> MS 1: To these ye Queen by Trumpets sound proclaims
> The Goddess now to grace the day proclaims
> The Goddess now by Hawkers Voice proclaims
> MS 2: The Goddess now by Hawkers Voice proclaims
> The herald Hawker's rusty Voice proclaims
> 1728: Now herald hawker's rusty voice proclaims
> 1729: . . . the Queen proclaims
> By herald hawkers, high, heroic Games.

The latest version in the First Broglio becomes, according to Richardson's transcriptions, the earliest in the Second. That reading remains virtually the same in the initial published edition, and it is changed to a form differing from all previous ones in the *Variorum*. Its collocation of "herald," "hawkers," and "rusty" had appeared first in the early manuscript: a couplet after 1.242 had read, "God save King T—— Grubstreet own our choice, / And Hawker Heralds roar with rusty Voice." Pope apparently noticed the repetition of "hawker" at the end of book 1 and start of book 2 and blended the former example into the latter, in the process reversing the words which would serve as noun and adjective. Indeed, the couplet from book 1 has disappeared from the second manuscript.

A passage in book 3 provides a different kind of evidence for the intervention of the Second Broglio between the first manuscript and the 1728 publication, rather than between the 1728 and 1729 editions. In Broglio 1, line 3.154 had cited Michael Maittaire, whom Sherburn identifies as "a learned protégé of the Oxfords" (*Corr.* 2:496n): "Concanen next, & Michel's rueful face!" Similarly, a passage near line 160 had read, "there musefull sitts Mattaire," phrasing repeated in the second manuscript. That couplet referring to Maittaire was deleted before the 1728 publication, and line 154 there appeared as "Lo H——ck's fierce, and M——'s rueful face!" "M——'s" could then be interpreted as "Mitchel's," as Broglio 2's version of 154 had it and as several keys speculated (others suggested "Milbourn" or "Maxwell"; in 1729 Pope changed the phrase to "Roome's funereal face"). When Pope wrote the earl of Oxford on 20 May 1728 about the *Dunciad*'s first appearance, he observed that "you'l see I have spar'd Mattaire at your request" (*Corr.* 2:496). Pope's intention to include Maittaire therefore changed before the 1728 publication. If the Second Broglio *followed* the 1728 edition, Pope would have reinserted the exact reference that he had previously deleted—an unattractive hypothesis for at least two reasons. Most importantly, it would mean that he reneged on his commitment to a close friend. The reincorporation would also entail an unusually tangled textual history of inclusion, deletion, reinclusion, a second deletion, and a return to the form that resulted from the first deletion (with subsequent modification of that form for the 1729 edition). Although such a pattern is not impossible, it is improbable in the face of the much simpler competing explanation.

The factors weighing against the Second Broglio preceding the 1728 *Dunciad* are substantial, but I believe none of them convincingly establishes that the manuscript instead followed that edition. As we have seen, Richardson's use of the 1736 *Dunciad* to record the readings means only that he did not copy them until at least 1736, not that the manuscript was necessarily prepared for that version—or, for that matter, for any edition of the *Variorum*. Of greater significance is the material for book 2 recorded on the flyleaf of the 1736 copy. The nearly five-dozen lines there begin with the eight verses that open the 1728 edition, continue with the ten that parallel the opening twelve of 1729, and conclude with a prose and verse outline of the royal levee that in 1742 was to appear in book 4. The connections with those later versions seem to have tempted commentators to argue for a late date, apparently on the assumption that Pope would use the lines shortly after composing them. But even by the most severe estimate, the levee passage did not see print for at least six years; by the most popular calculation, based on the hypothesis that the manuscript was prepared for the 1729 edition, the wait was thirteen years. In this light an additional year of delay would seem insignificant and not rule out the existence of the text before 1728.

The similarity with opening lines of the *Variorum* suggests chronological proximity of the manuscript and that version, but only two full lines and parts of two others actually appear there. The manuscript passage contains the introductions for both the 1728 and 1729 versions of book 2; regardless of which edition the manuscript immediately preceded, Pope would have chosen to keep one set of lines and to reject the other. To emphasize the connection with the 1729 edition is therefore unjustified, for the parallel with the 1728 one is equally important. It was not uncommon, moreover, for Pope to reclaim material that he had earlier worked up but not printed. Such was the case with the verses from his youth discussed earlier; his utilization of the levee passage provides another striking example. One of the themes of Mack's discussions of Pope's manuscripts is in fact that Pope often went back to materials drawn up for earlier poems. That practice also helps to explain why he saved his manuscripts, and why he put Richardson through the trouble of collating them.

The argument that the textual history of any of Pope's works zigzags rather than proceeds directly to the finished form might be seen to work against the notion that both *Dunciad* manuscripts came before 1728: Pope was certainly capable of returning to early readings (as in the Second Broglio) even after he had excluded them (as in the 1728 edition), and then rejecting them a second time as he produced a text that closely resembled what he constructed after the first rejection (i.e.,

The Annotations

the 1729 version). Even the chronology I am proposing illustrated something of that process. The first manuscript's reading of the third line of book 1, "I sing; say great ones (You these works inspire)," metamorphosed into "Say great *Patricians!* (since yourselves inspire" in the 1728 edition and into a form almost identical in 1729. The line in the 1743 *Dunciad in Four Books*, however, reappeared with overtones of its early form: "I sing. Say you, her instruments the Great!" Nonetheless, there is no evidence that Pope ever extended to entire poems this treatment of individual words and passages, and the flat statement that Pope would reuse earlier materials needs to be carefully qualified. To repeat: I think it unlikely that Pope completely rejected *The Dunciad* as it was first printed and that he then wrote out the entire poem in a version which in relatively insubstantial ways modified that of his earlier manuscript.

The most troublesome obstacles to the argument that both manuscripts antedate 1728 arise from their prose notes. In its transcription of a passage in book 2, *The Last and Greatest Art* (140) records from the Second Broglio that Edmund Curll stood in the pillory in February 1728/9, which would be nine months after the first *Dunciad*. Moreover, in the 1736 copy containing the readings from that manuscript, Richardson has modified some of the notes of the *Variorum* text. He thereby implies that the full notes, in a sometimes variant form, were already present in the manuscript.

What first appears to be the more intractable point, the date of Curll's punishment, resolves easily: "1728/9" is a mistranscription of the date Richardson actually wrote, "1727/8," and the citation is consistent with the date he recorded a few pages earlier for the same event (*Art*, 138). That correction also helps to fix more clearly a date at which Pope was working on the Second Broglio: after late February and, if the argument that the manuscript preceded the printed form is correct, before mid May of 1728. The note seems not to have appeared until the second manuscript; there is, at least, no record of it at the first of the comparable passages in Broglio 1 (at the site of the second possible occurrence Richardson says that a large section of that manuscript is "torn out").

In pondering the second problem raised by the notes, it is well to begin by considering several of their features. The earlier manuscript, which is commonly agreed to come before 1728, contains fourteen notes, mostly identifying classical parallels. The 1728 edition itself has nineteen, but it uses none of the manuscript ones. Secondly, the 1729 *Variorum* picks up fewer than half of the approximately three-dozen sources and annotations found in the second manuscript, and it revises drastically those it does employ. Conversely, only a tiny fraction of the notes that do occur in the *Variorum*, where they often dominate the page even though they are printed in smaller type, appear in the second manuscript.

What seems to be the case is that Pope recorded parallels and composed explanatory annotations unsystematically as he went. Gradually he seems to have recognized the value of providing an extensive list especially of his sources; hence the greater number in the second manuscript than in the first. But once he conceived of the culmination of this strategy in the form of the *Variorum* (planned, as we have seen, by the time of the 1728 publication), he apparently decided to postpone most of the notes for that heavily laden edition, in order to make its contrast with the earlier one all the more striking. Many of his manuscript notations were in the form of what Swift had called "hints" that could be expanded later. Hence the ending of some of them with "&c.," as at 1.54 in the first manuscript; hence also the explanation of why those he did draw on were often significantly shorter in manuscript than eventually in print.

The key to understanding Richardson's relatively few alterations to the notes of the 1736 edition seems to be that he treated his manuscript materials in different ways. As we shall see shortly, he clearly did this with lines of verse, representing poetic passages absent from the printed edition differently

The Annotations

from those that did appear there but in modified form. A similar principle appears to hold for the prose notes. On the one hand, it is easy to identify his different practices in presenting this material. Sometimes, acting as an editor, he connects manuscript and printed passages for the reader, as when he writes at 1.29 in his transcription of Broglio 2, "See Note 106" (of the 1736 text). Usually he simply places the note in the margin, without indicating how it relates to the adjacent published version. In only five instances does he actually mark the printed notes to indicate alterations. To determine the meaning of those practices is more difficult—but, I believe, largely possible.

I surmise first of all that Richardson, like modern editors, viewed the prose notes differently from the poetic text. He seems to have been thorough in recording discrepancies in verse between manuscript and edition, but it is difficult to believe that he was equally conscientious with prose, especially concerning elements present in print but not in manuscript. Although it is difficult to gain from the standard modern edition a sense of Pope's alterations in his notes through successive versions (the policy of the Twickenham editor was to identify only those textual revisions that have "any claim to importance" [5:6]), collation reveals that Pope tinkered with the prose as much as with the poetry. It is therefore implausible that an early manuscript which varied considerably in its poetic text from Richardson's 1736 copy—the fifth authorized edition of the *Variorum*—differed in prose matters only three-dozen times. Richardson's failure to indicate the relationship between the manuscript and most of the prose may on occasion signal that the two were identical, but I suspect that usually he considered only the notes that were present in the manuscript, thereby ignoring the vast material of 1736 not found in the holograph. He would have recorded material chiefly in two ways: marginal notes alone for manuscript notes not printed at all or else printed in drastically modified form; and marginal notes along with markings in the printed text for readings where the changes were brief enough to be conveniently recorded. When he modifies 1736 notes, therefore, he does not mean to intimate that the remaining material existed in Broglio 2 but rather to indicate chiefly that the Second Broglio had readings not found in the later printed text. His system of notations in the 1736 volume therefore does not necessarily imply that he was working from a manuscript that formed the basis for an edition of the *Variorum*.

Because Richardson's copy of the first octavo now in the Huntington Library also contains annotations, it is worth considering what relationship that record might bear to the manuscript history of the poem. As observed earlier, the title page has the notation "[N. All here added or changd is from a Copy of Mr Popes of this same Edition.] / *1777*"; the ink is different from that for Richardson's adjacent signature. Though the statement is dated five years after Richardson's death and obviously is not his, it most likely is based on his authority, and he probably had received this copy along with the others from Pope. The volume's notes signal alterations in only four-dozen passages: some fill the blanks of names, a few modify words or even whole lines, but more than half consist only of a vertical line or "x" in the margin. What is tantalizing is that roughly half the markings occur in passages Richardson describes as "torn out" in the manuscript he collates in the other 1728 octavo. (Appendix 5 identifies the "torn out" sections and records the Huntington notes.)

But that coincidence seems without special significance. Collation reveals that nearly all the marked passages were changed for the 1729 *Variorum*; notes near the beginnings of books 1 and 2, for example, indicate where the inscription to Swift and a new beginning were added. Of the seven instances not altered in 1729, all but two or three were modified to the suggested reading by the editions of 1735. On the other hand, only a small percentage of the cases in which the 1729 edition differs from the 1728 are marked. Only once does a reading here match one in Richardson's other two *Dunciad* transcriptions.

The Annotations

What seems to be the situation is that these marks represent a collation, probably done by Richardson for Pope, of changes Pope made for editions subsequent to 1728. Richardson could have gathered them all from printed texts, just as for the 1735 *Works II* volume he identified variations in published forms of several *Epistles*. But two mysteries remain: why the notes record a couple of readings not found in any published form, and why the list of alterations is so sparse. With the hope that placing the annotations on record may help resolve these questions, I have registered them in Appendix 5.

With the Broglio manuscripts themselves made accessible and their relationship ascertained, critics can assess their significance as well. Maynard Mack in particular has begun that work, notably in *Collected in Himself* (339–43) and in the introduction to his transcriptions in *The Last and Greatest Art* (97–100). He points out the exuberance that Pope had to tone down for print, explores the motivations for name changes in the developing forms, and pays special attention to the "skeleton plan of most of *Dunciad* IV" present in the second manuscript "before publication of the 1729 edition." If the present assessment of the connection of the First and Second Broglio is correct, that plan existed earlier yet—and requires even greater qualification of the assertion by Pope's editor William Warburton that Pope "had concerted the plan of the fourth book of the Dunciad with the Editor" in 1740 or 1741.[29]

In the manuscripts we see the basis for Pope's statement in 1728 that the names of the dunces were clapped in as they arose, how the nature of the appellations shifts (as Tryphon becomes identifiable as Tonson, for instance, in book 2), or how the use of initials and blanks reflects Pope's intention as it represents a calculated ambiguity after he has labeled the targets unmistakably in the drafts. We see Pope's indecisiveness about making the political satire explicit as he sometimes emphasizes such allusions ("And when a Settle falls a Tibbalds

---

29. Warburton's note on 9:348 of the large octavo edition of Pope's *Works*, 1751.

reigns" in 1.5 becomes "Still *Dunce the second reigns like Dunce the first*") and on other occasions submerges them (at 1.244, "And near our Monarch Dullness fix her throne" shifts to "Till *Albion*, as *Hibernia*, bless my throne"). We can also watch Pope restrain his early bawdiness, as in the tickling contest in book 2. A version in the first manuscript read:

> A Nicer part shy W———r chose to probe,
> Latent beneath ye Cinctures of his Robe.
> This well observd, unheeded by the rest,
> He brought his Sister, & she tickled best.
> So taught by *Venus*, *Paris* learnt the art
> To touch thy only penetrable part.

By the time it reached print the passage remained indecorous, but its unseemliness was now disguised so that responsibility for such an interpretation became largely the reader's:

> the *Queen* of *Love*
> His Sister sends, her vot'ress, from above.
> As taught by *Venus*, *Paris* learnt the art
> To touch *Achilles*' only tender part.   (196–99)

By scrutinizing Pope's embryonic notes we can recognize parallels that have hitherto escaped attention—especially, in the First Broglio, to the *Aeneid*, but also to Persius and Homer (and to still others, including English authors such as Shakespeare, in the second manuscript). Within the past few years a critic has published his observation of Pope's indebtedness to Addison at 3.214 (*TE* 3.260), the late eighteenth-century editor Gilbert Wakefield first spotted the allusion to Ovid's *Metamorphoses* at 2.61 (*TE* 2.73), and the Twickenham editor seems to claim originality for identifying official positions of Burnet and Duckett at 3.142 (*TE* 3.180). Although Pope never printed these references, the Second Broglio listed each of them.

The manuscripts (for present purposes, the First Broglio in particular) also reveal many passages of poetry that Pope discarded as the poem progressed, notably on pages 36 through

The Annotations

42. The facsimile is especially useful in making clear the connections between these passages as Richardson has transcribed them. These documents further show, as Pope's biographer Owen Ruffhead reported, why Pope "used himself to say, that . . . [book 2] of his poem cost him most trouble, and pleased him least"—not simply because of Ruffhead's explanation that Pope here "was doing violence to his nicer feelings" but rather because Pope could not settle on a version or get the parts to cohere in a suitable manner (370). The overall advantage of the manuscripts then is that they provide insight into the development of Pope's verse. With that comes the realization that the *Dunciad* of 1728 was part of a long and laborious process of composition; this contestant in the War of the Dunces hardly sprang fully armed from the head of Zeus.

One task remains: to provide some guidance in interpreting Richardson's collations. The first necessity is to identify features that cannot be determined from the photographs, especially passages written in other than the dark brown or black ink used for most of the volume. Several notes are in pencil, as well as in a different script: those at the bottom of the title, the lines in the right margin of page 11, and apparently the names "Collins" (overwritten in ink) and "Tolland" to the right of 2.353 on page 33. In the facsimile the second line above "Tolland" appears to be struck through, but here the words "tho prepar'd to" are written over what seemingly is a long pencil stroke. Immediately above that stands a solitary capital letter, possibly a "T" or "J"; it too seems to be written in ink over pencil.

The note on the title is rubbed and is not completely decipherable. It appears to read, 'Hic Stilus haud petet ult. / Quemquā [two lines totaling 60 mm] at ille / Qui me comórit, Melius non tangere cla[mo] / Flebit, & infignis tota contabitur urbe. / Hor Sat. 2.1.39'. Pope imitates these verses (39–40 and 44–46 in Horace) in his "First Satire of the Second Book of Horace," lines 69–70 and 76–80 (*TE* 4:10–13) as he explains that he satirizes only when provoked. On page 11, the manuscript note is: 'Vinctus mitte/ris Jllerdam / Hor Ep.' The passage is from Horace's Epistle 1.20.13, where he describes the fate of printed sheets used as covers to letters sent to the provinces.

The ink of the vertical lines bracketing text at the bottom of pages 18, 19, 46, and 47 and at the top of 46 now appears as red. In book 2, about a dozen names that fill blanks from pages 28 through 35 are browner than the rest. Nearly all of these occur in a section for which Richardson says the manuscript is "torn out"; the readings are obvious ones and represent safe inferences. The words written in this different ink, and usually in a slightly larger hand, are: "Hungerford" (line 242), "weekly" (256), "Dennis" (259), "Eusden" (267), "Welstead" (281), "Eusden" (288), "Shadwell" (310), "Milbourn" (311), "Henley's" (324), "Centlivre" (365), and "Eusden" (379), as well as the word "add" and the vertical line before 357–58.

Several words are written over others. In the fourth line of notes at the bottom of page 26, "Nature" is across something indistinguishable. In line four at the bottom of 27, "who" is over "that". To the right of 2.353 on page 33, "Ev'n thou," overwrites the penciled "Collins"; besides the other overwriting cited there, the line immediately above "Tolland" that reads "ever prompt to" is almost totally obscured by a series of continuous loops. At 2.355, the symbol immediately preceding the line and the second word after the verse seem intentionally struck out and are unrecoverable. Also on 33, in the notes four lines from the bottom, "V" and "o" of "Voice" overwrite a couple of letters, the first of which is probably "h". In the first line of notes after the text on 42, the final letters of "Who" overwrite something, and the words "& bath" which immediately follow seem to be partially erased.

In reconstructing the manuscript from Richardson's notes, the obvious but crucial principle to keep in mind is that the printed text is later than the manuscript he is working with. Richardson usually indicates variations from the print by underscoring with dashes the words that earlier read differ-

The Annotations

ently. Usually he then records the previous text immediately above the underscored phrase. Sometimes a passage has gone through several revisions; often in such cases the spatial arrangement of the annotations proves significant. Richardson tends to place the latest manuscript reading above the printed line, the previous one in a side margin, and the one before that at the foot of the page (sometimes continuing that reading at the head or at right angles in the side margins). If there is still too much text for the page to accommodate, he will move to the facing page—or, as at 2.215, to blank leaves such as the title-page verso or the half title. When he copies long sections that do not match any of the extant text, he sometimes reverses his basic procedure: on the title-page verso, for instance, he specifies that the lines constituting the central paragraphs are those that were "first writ," and that the readings in the margins are now the corrections, or *later* forms. What these opposite policies have in common is Richardson's adoption of the method that requires the least interpretation and transcription on his part—with the result of maximum accuracy, one suspects and hopes. A problem arises in determining which practice he is employing when in the margins of an ordinary page he copies variant manuscript passages that also contain further alterations. Although the system here might be presumed to be the same as for other material on such pages (i.e., that modifications of what for the moment is the base text signify earlier readings), my own collation of his First and Second Broglio transcriptions indicates that, if one assumes that Broglio 2 readings hold a logically continuous position between Broglio 1 and the 1728 text, Richardson often instead follows the pattern of having alterations signal later readings, a method that he explicitly announces only on the title-page verso.

As part of his record Richardson employs a system of symbols in the margin. The most obvious are a caret to mark insertion and a delta to signal deletion. The logic of these signs may seem to be reversed, however, and again it is critical to keep his basic method in mind. A delta beside a passage of printed text indicates that the lines have been *added* for that text. Given Richardson's practice of working backwards to progressively earlier states of the text, a delta signifies that the passage is absent (and only in this sense "deleted") in the *previous* version. In the same way, the caret means that the earlier version had additional material, which Richardson then prints elsewhere in the margin. In short: a delta means that the later form will be the longer, and a caret indicates that the later one will be the shorter. Or to put it another way: a delta means that longer is later, a caret that longer is earlier.

The other symbols are less confusing. Richardson uses the symbol "x" as a footnote marker; it cross-refers to material elsewhere in the transcription. Occasionally he places arabic numbers (as high as "4") in front of verses to indicate their original order with respect to each other. The abbreviations "inf[ra]" and "sup[ra]" point to material below or above on a particular page or in the poetic text. A bracket or vertical line in the left margin specifies the verses affected by one of the other symbols. When placed along the printed text, such a line without an accompanying symbol seems to indicate that the passage was added after the inscription of the manuscript had ceased. That is, it implies the presence of a delta and means that these lines were missing in the previous version. Occasionally Richardson will place a vertical rule (|) between two readings; he thereby seems to indicate that Pope had not yet chosen which possibility to adopt, although the symbol may indicate his own indecisiveness about which choice was the earlier.

Richardson's habit of filling in names in the sections where he says the manuscript is missing prompts the salutary reminder that his version of the First Broglio is an edited one. And as Professor Mack notes in his own transcriptions of the collations, Richardson's pen occasionally slips. Although his record is strikingly self-consistent and implicitly reliable, especially those who themselves have collated will recognize the need to maintain the traditional spirit of scholarly questioning when using his work.

Works Cited

Allibone, Samuel A. *A Critical Dictionary of English Literature*. 3 vols. Philadelphia: Childs and Peterson (vol. 1), Lippincott (vols. 2–3), 1858–71.
Boswell, James. *Life of Johnson*. Edited by R. W. Chapman. 3d ed., corrected by J. D. Fleeman. London: Oxford Univ. Press, 1970.
British Museum. Department of Prints and Drawings. *Catalogue of Prints and Drawings in the British Museum. Division I. Political and Personal Satires*. 11 vols. London: British Museum, 1870–1954.
Butt, John. "Pope's Poetical Manuscripts." *Proceedings of the British Academy* 40 (1954): 23–29.
Carruthers, Robert. *The Life of Alexander Pope*. 2d ed. London: Henry G. Bohn, 1857.
Chandler, W. K. "The First Edition of the *Dunciad*." *Modern Philology* 29 (1931): 59–72.
[Curll, Edmund.] *A Compleat Key to the Dunciad*. London: Printed for A. Dodd, 1728. 2d and 3d eds., London: Printed for E. Curll, 1728.
———. *The Curliad*. London: Printed for the Author, 1729.
Dennis, John. *Reflections Critical and Satyrical, Upon a Late Rhapsody, Call'd, An Essay Upon Criticism*. London: Printed for Bernard Lintott, [1711].
———. *Remarks Upon Several Passages in the Preliminaries to the Dunciad*. London: Printed for H. Whitridge, 1729.
F. G. "Inventory of Pope's Goods Taken after His Death." *Notes and Queries*, 6th ser. 5 (13 May 1882): 363–65.
Fielding, Henry. *The Convent-Garden Journal and A Plan of the Universal Register-Office*. Edited by Bertrand A. Goldgar. The Wesleyan Edition of the Works of Henry Fielding. Middletown, Conn.: Wesleyan Univ. Press, 1988.
Foxon, David. "Two Cruces in Pope Bibliography." *Times Literary Supplement*, 24 Jan. 1958, 52.

———. *English Verse 1701–1750*. 2 vols. London: Cambridge Univ. Press, 1975.

———. "Pope and the Early Eighteenth-Century Book-Trade." The Lyell Lectures, Oxford, 1976. Typescript in British Library.

Griffith, Reginald H. "The *Dunciad* of 1728." *Modern Philology* 13 (1915): 1–18.

———. *Alexander Pope: A Bibliography*. 1 vol. in 2 parts. 1922–27. Reprint. London: Holland Press, 1968.

———. "The Dunciad Duodecimo." *Colophon*, n.s. 3, no. 4 (1938): 569–86.

Grundy, Isobel M. "New Verse by Henry Fielding." *PMLA* 87 (1972): 213–45.

Guerinot, J. V. *Pamphlet Attacks on Alexander Pope 1711–1744: A Descriptive Bibliography*. New York: New York Univ. Press, 1969.

Heartman, Charles F. "George D. Smith, 1870–1920: Gentleman Bookseller." *American Book Collector* 23, no. 5 (May–June 1973): 3–26.

Johnson, Samuel. *Lives of the English Poets*. Edited by George Birkbeck Hill. 3 vols. Oxford: Clarendon, 1905.

Laus Ululae. The Praise of Owls. In *Miscellanea. In Two Volumes*, vol. 2. London: Printed in the Year, 1727 [1726].

Leranbaum, Miriam. *Alexander Pope's 'Opus Magnum' 1729–1744*. Oxford: Clarendon, 1977.

Lounsbury, Thomas R. *The Text of Shakespeare*. New York: Charles Scribner's Sons, 1906. Published in London as *The First Editors of Shakespeare (Pope and Theobald)*.

Mack, Maynard. *Collected in Himself: Essays Critical, Biographical, and Bibliographical on Pope and Some of His Contemporaries*. Newark: Univ. of Delaware Press, 1982.

———. *The Last and Greatest Art: Some Unpublished Poetical Manuscripts of Alexander Pope*. Newark: Univ. of Delaware Press, 1984.

———. *Alexander Pope: A Life*. New York: Norton; New Haven: Yale Univ. Press, 1985.

McKenzie, Alan T. "The Solemn Owl and the Laden Ass: The Iconography of the Frontispieces to *The Dunciad*." *Harvard Library Bulletin* 24 (1976): 25–39.

McLaverty, James. Review of *The Last and Greatest Art*, by Maynard Mack. *Analytical and Enumerative Bibliography*, n.s. 1 (1987): 84–89.

Mengel, Elias F., Jr. "The *Dunciad* Illustrations." *Eighteenth-Century Studies* 7 (1973–74): 161–78.

Works Cited

Mumby, Frank A. *Publishing and Bookselling.* New York: Bowker, 1931.

Munby, A. N. L., and Lenore Coral. *British Book Sale Catalogues 1676–1800: A Union List.* London: Mansell, 1977.

Negus, Samuel. *A compleat and private List of all the Printing-houses in and about the Cities of London and Westminster* (1724). In Nichols, *Literary Anecdotes,* 1:288–312.

Nichols, John. *Literary Anecdotes of the Eighteenth Century.* 9 vols. London: Printed for the Author, 1812–16.

"Notes on Sales." *Times Literary Supplement,* 8 Jan. 1938, 32.

Pope, Alexander. *The Works of Alexander Pope.* Edited by William Warburton. 9 vols., large octavo. London: Printed for J. & P. Knapton et al., 1751.

———. *The Works of Alexander Pope.* Edited by Joseph Warton. 9 vols. London: Printed for B. Law et al., 1797.

———. *The Works of Alexander Pope.* 9 vols. Basel: Printed and sold by J. J. Tourneisen, 1803.

———. *The Works of Alexander Pope.* Edited by William Lisle Bowles. 10 vols. London: Printed for J. Johnson et al., 1806.

———. *The Works of Alexander Pope.* 8 vols. London: Printed for Nichols and Son et al., 1812.

———. *The Works of Alexander Pope.* Edited by Whitwell Elwin and William John Courthope. 10 vols. London: John Murray, 1871–86. Vol. 4, *Poetry* (including *The Dunciad*), 1882.

———. *The Poetical Works of Alexander Pope.* New York: Thomas Y. Crowell, [1896].

———. *The Dunciad: An Heroic Poem, 1728.* Oxford: Clarendon, 1928.

———. *The Twickenham Edition of the Poems of Alexander Pope.* John Butt, General Editor. 11 vols. in 12. London: Methuen; New Haven: Yale Univ. Press, 1939–69. Vol. 3, pt. 2, *An Essay on Man.* Edited by Maynard Mack, 1950. Vol. 4, *Imitations of Horace.* Edited by John Butt, 1939; 3d ed., 1961. Vol. 5, *The Dunciad.* Edited by James Sutherland, 1943; 3d ed., 1963. Vol. 6, *Minor Poems.* Edited by Norman Ault and John Butt, 1954.

———. *The Correspondence of Alexander Pope.* Edited by George Sherburn. 5 vols. Oxford: Clarendon, 1956.

———, and Jonathan Swift. *Miscellanies. The Third Volume.* London: Printed for Benj. Motte and Lawton Gilliver, 1732.

Pope Commemoration, 1888. Loan Museum. Catalogue of the Books, Autographs, Paintings, Drawings, Engravings, and Personal Relics, Ex-

hibited in the Town Hall, Twickenham, July 31st to August 4th, 1888. Richmond: Edward King, 1888.

[Ralph, James.] *Sawney. An Heroic Poem.* London: Printed and Sold by J. Roberts, 1728.

Ricci, Seymour de. *English Collectors of Books & Manuscripts (1530–1930) and Their Marks of Ownership.* New York: Macmillan; Cambridge: Cambridge Univ. Press, 1930.

Richardson, Jonathan, Sr., and Jonathan Richardson, Jr. *Explanatory Notes and Remarks on Milton's Paradise Lost.* London: Printed for James, John, and Paul Knapton, 1734.

Richardson, Jonathan, Jr., *Richardsoniana.* London: Printed for J. Dodsley, 1776.

Rogers, Robert W. *The Major Satires of Alexander Pope.* Illinois Studies in Language and Literature, vol. 40. Urbana: Univ. of Illinois Press, 1955.

Ruffhead, Owen. *The Life of Alexander Pope, Esq.* Octavo. London: Printed for C. Bathurst et al., 1769.

Savage, Richard. *A Collection of Pieces in Verse and Prose, Which have been publish'd on Occasion of the Dunciad.* London: Printed for L. Gilliver, 1732.

Schmitz, Robert M. *Pope's Essay on Criticism 1709: A Study of the Bodleian Manuscript Text with Facsimiles, Transcripts, and Variants.* St. Louis: Washington Univ. Press, 1962.

Sherburn, George. "Aids to Readers: The Dunciad." In *Selections from Alexander Pope*, edited by Sherburn, 450–58. Nelson's English Series. New York: Thomas Nelson & Sons, 1929.

———. "New Anecdotes about Alexander Pope." *Notes and Queries* 203 (1958): 343–49.

———. "Pope at Work." In *Essays on the Eighteenth Century Presented to David Nichol Smith in Honour of His Seventieth Birthday.* Edited by J[ames] S[utherland] and F. P. W[ilson]. Oxford: Clarendon, 1945.

Solly, Edward. "Pope and Dryden." *Notes and Queries*, 6th ser. 12 (17 Oct. 1885): 301.

Spence, Joseph. *Observations, Anecdotes, and Characters of Books and Men.* Edited by James M. Osborn. 2 vols. Oxford: Clarendon, 1966.

Stowe, Harriet Beecher. *A Key to Uncle Tom's Cabin.* Boston: John P. Jewett, 1853.

Swift, Jonathan. *The Correspondence of Jonathan Swift.* Edited by Harold Williams. 5 vols. Oxford: Clarendon, 1963.

Swift, Jonathan, and Alexander Pope. *Miscellanies. The Third Volume.* London: Printed for Benj. Motte and Lawton Gilliver, 1732.

Works Cited

Tanselle, G. Thomas. "Textual Scholarship." In *Introduction to Scholarship in Modern Languages and Literatures*, edited by Joseph Gibaldi, 29–52. New York: MLA, 1981.
Theobald, Lewis. *Shakespeare Restored*. London: Printed for R. Francklin et al., 1726.
Tracy, Clarence. *The Artificial Bastard: A Biography of Richard Savage*. Toronto: Univ. of Toronto Press, 1953.
Vander Meulen, David L. "The Printing of Pope's *Dunciad*, 1728." *Studies in Bibliography* 35 (1982): 271–85.
Wimsatt, William K. *The Portraits of Alexander Pope*. New Haven: Yale Univ. Press, 1965.
Wise, Thomas J. *The Ashley Library*. 11 vols. London: Printed for Private Circulation, 1922–36.
———. *A Pope Library*. 1931. Reprint with new introd. by K. I. D. Maslen. Folkestone and London: Dawsons, 1973.
Wycherley, William. *The Posthumous Works of William Wycherley, Esq; In Prose and Verse*. 2 vols. Vol. 1, edited by Lewis Theobald. London: Printed for A. Bettesworth et al., 1728. Vol. 2, edited by Alexander Pope. London: Printed for J. Roberts, 1729.
Young, Edward. *The Correspondence of Edward Young, 1683–1765*. Edited by Henry Pettit. Oxford: Clarendon, 1971.

THE
DUNCIAD
of 1728

A Facsimile

Pope

THE PUBLISHER TO THE READER.

IT will be found a true observation, tho' somewhat surprizing, that when any scandal is vented against a man of the highest distinction and character either in the State or in Literature, the publick in general afford it a most quiet reception, and the larger part accept it as favourably as if it were some kindness done to themselves: Whereas if a known scoundrel or blockhead chance to be but touch'd upon, a whole legion is up in Arms, and it becomes the common Cause of all Scriblers, Booksellers, and Printers whatsoever.

Not to search too deeply into the reason hereof, I will only observe as a Fact, that every week for these two Months past, the town has been persecuted

cuted with Pamphlets, Advertisements, Letters, and weekly Essays, not only against the Wit and Writings, but against the Character and Person, of Mr. Pope. And that of all those men who have received pleasure from his Writings (which by modest computation may be about a hundred thousand in these Kingdoms of England *and* Ireland, *not to mention* Jersey, Guernsey, *the* Orcades, *those in the* New world, *and* Foreigners *who have translated him into their languages) of all this number, not a man hath stood up to say one word in his defence.*

The only exception is the Author of the following Poem, who doubtless had either a better insight into the grounds of this clamour, or a better opinion of Mr. Pope's *integrity, join'd with a greater personal love for him, than any other of his numerous friends and admirers.*

Further, that he was in his peculiar intimacy, appears from the knowledge he manifests of the most private Authors of all the anonymous pieces against him, and from his having in this Poem attacked no man living, who had not before printed and published against this particular Gentleman.

How I became possest of it, is of no concern to the

the Reader; but it would have been a wrong to him, had I detain'd this publication: since those Names which are its chief ornaments, die off daily so fast, as must render it too soon unintelligible. If it permittes the Author to give us a more perfect edition, I have my end.

Who he is, I cannot say, and (which is great pity) there is certainly nothing in his style and manner of writing, which can distinguish, or discover him. For if it bears any resemblance to that of Mr. P. 'tis not improbable but it might be done on purpose, with a view to have it pass for his. But by the frequency of his allusions to Virgil, and a labour'd, (not to say affected, shortness, in imitation of him, I should think him more an admirer of the Roman Poet than of the Grecian, and in that, not of the same taste with his Friend.

I have been well inform'd, that this work was the labour of full six years of his life, and that he retired himself entirely from all the avocations and pleasures of the world, to attend diligently to its correction and perfection; and six years more he intended to bestow upon it, as it should seem by this verse of Statius, which was cited at the head of his manuscript.

Oh

Oh mihi biffenos multum vigilata per annos, Duncia!———

Hence also we learn the true Title *of the Poem; which with the same certainty as we call that of* Homer *the* Iliad, *of* Virgil *the* Æneid, *of* Camoens *the* Lusiad, *of* Voltaire *the* Henriad, *we may pronounce could have been, and can be no other, than*

The DUNCIAD.

It is styled Heroic, as being doubly so; not only with respect to its nature, which according to the best Rules of the Ancients and strictest ideas of the Moderns, is critically such; but also with regard to the Heroical disposition and high courage of the Writer, who dar'd to stir up such a formidable, irritable, and implacable race of mortals.

The time and date of the Action is evidently in the last reign, when the office of City Poet expir'd upon the death of Elkanah Settle, *and he has fix'd it to the Mayoralty of Sir* Geo. Tho———ld. *But there may arise some*

some obscurity in Chronology from the Names in the Poem, by the inevitable removal of some Authors, and Insertion of others, in their Niches. For whoever will consider the unity of the whole design, will be sensible, that the Poem was not made for these Authors, but these Authors for the Poem. And I should judge they were clapp'd in as they rose, fresh and fresh, and chang'd from day to day, in like manner as when the old boughs wither, we thrust new ones into a chimney.

I would not have the reader too much troubled or anxious, if he cannot decypher them; since when he shall have found them out, he will probably know no more of the Persons than before.

Yet we judg'd it better to preserve them as they are, than to change them for fictitious names, by which the Satyr would only be multiplied; and applied to many instead of one. Had the Hero, for instance, been called Codrus, how many would have affirm'd him to be Mr. W——— Mr. D——— Sir R——— B———, &c. but now, all that unjust scandal is saved, by calling him Theobald, which by good luck happens to be the name of a real person.

4 Vociferation.

viii The PUBLISHER, &c.

I am indeed aware, that this name may to some appear too mean, for the Hero of an Epic Poem? But it is hoped, they will alter that opinion, when they find, that an Author no less eminent than la Bruyere, has thought him worthy a place in his Characters.

Voudriez vous, THEOBALDE, que je crusse que vous êtes baisse? que vous n'êtes plus Poete, ni bel esprit? que vous êtes presentement aussi *Mauvais juge de tout genre d'Ouvrage,* que *Mechant Auteur?* Votre air libre & presumptueux me rassure, & me persuade tout le contraire. &c. *Characteres,* Vol. I. de la Societe & de la Conversation, pag. 176. Edit. Amst. 1720.

+ young & fair.

With scornfull smile at this the Hag reveals
The brindled Monster in her Robe conceal'd
When thus ye Hag: now blush ye Prepossest;
Lo! here ye Cat I suckled at my Breast:
Well have ye Judg'd — then scornfull she reveals
The brindled Monster in her Robe conceal'd — own. as MS. 2 in
Now thousand Tongues — as it. 115. corrected
Ed.ᵗ 1736. p. 151.]

[Note. This, & page but one after, what was in 1 Edit p. 26 &c. The tor of Reverse
ll. 201. Now turn to different Sports (y Goddess crys) &c (ye like page is between)]

And learn my Sons ye wondrous Powr of Noise.
Who fail to ravish or to Steal the Heart — To move, to raise, to ravish ev'ry
With Shakespear's Nature, or with Johnson's Art
Can wake ye Sense & terrify ye Soul   Hard task! yet fail we not to shake
With grumbling Thunders from ye Mustard bowl.   Discharg'd? Displod?
With Horns & Trumpets to wild Fury swell, The Mind to Madness w French Horns w
Or sink in Sorrows by a Tolling Bell: And now   with
These happy Arts Attention can comand,   Such
When Fancy flags & Sense is at a Stand. Tho'
Try then new airs whose feebly plaining tones   Try new ones then, the Sol
Match the then Muse of ye Cat that whines: calls be ye bribe
Or try this Drum whose   Of him whose Chatter shames
And who can join his hoarse Heroic Base   ye Monkey tribe.
Or ye Clarion of the loud Trumpet of the Braying Ass.   Now thousand tongues &c
Two Slipshod Muses pac'd sedate before, ye Skrong?
With Heads unpin'd but meditating Song.   Disordered Hairs
Locks decompos'd as starting from a Dream
And never wash'd but in Castalia's Stream.
First in thin treble Infantine I sow,   In feeble
Or plaintive hules, like kindest Kitten's Woe;
Now strains ye tenor to a sharper squall,
Now mewing melts in mimic a dying fall.
More Tragic N——n swells with deeper Rage, But then
Like the base murmur of Grimalkin's age.
But who, alass! for fifty five declare?   In vain! small fair Nymphs do so shar
Each that gave Sentence for the young & fair!   All gave ye Suffrage to
Then swells
Harmonic
As when the Long-eard mothers milk'd before   ee'r day ye Milky mothers wa
The gouty miser's triple-bolted Door   at some Sick   gain
For her defrauded absent   makes   their   Fools they
A cry so loud that all the Guild awakes. moan   Children mu
Jove sighs St Gilbert, starting at ye Bray,
From dreams of Millions, & a groat to pay:
Such chatter rises;   ass intones to ass,   So swells each Wind-pipe;
Harmonic twang of Leather, Horn & Brass such as trumpets —L. 1. ll.237
But high o'er all Sonorous Blackmore's Strain   far
Street, walls & Skies bray back to Him again
In Tuthill feilds the Asses in amaze
Prick all their Ears, & wondring cease to graze
From George's feilds Thames wafts it thro' to Rufus' —
Heav'n takes his Praises and Hungerford recho's
Confess'd Supreme in both ye Powrs of Song.   With Blackmore Blackmu
None sung so loudly & none sung so Long.   Shouts th'applauding Throng
                                                Who Sings so loudly & who
                                                  sings so long.
                                               Diving IN ye Leaf love oo
                                               lo v. 319. slow mov'd

THE
DUNCIAD
IN
THREE BOOKS.

THE DUNCIAD.

BOOK the FIRST.

N. The Title was torn off on purpose.

An Heroic Poem.

BOOK and the man I sing, the first who *who first from Grubstreet*
brings *Courts*
The *Smithfield* muses to the ears of kings.
Say great Patricians! (since yourselves inspire
These wond'rous works; so *Jove* and fate require!)
5 Say from what cause, ~~in vain decry'd and curst,~~ *tho so*
Still † *Dunce the second reigns like Dunce the first?*
In eldest time, e'er mortals writ or read,
E'er *Pallas* issued from the Thund'rer's head,
          Dulness *Hence*

† *Dryd.*

1.3. I sing; say great ones (you these works inspire)
Since this Joves will, & Brittains fate require)
× *Say what the Cause that still this taste remains,*
And when a Settle falls a Tibbalds reigns?

× *Why, from what cause, th' Immortal Race remains,*

2   The DUNCIAD.

Dulness o'er all possess'd her antient right,
10 Daughter of *Chaos* and eternal *Night*:
Fate in their dotage this fair idiot gave,
Gross as her sire, and as her mother grave,
Laborious, heavy, busy, bold, and blind,
She rul'd, in native anarchy, the mind.

lost restore 15 Still her old empire to confirm, she tries,
For born a Goddess, *Dulness* never dies.

Where wave the tatter'd ensigns of *Rag-Fair*,
seems to nod A yawning ruin hangs and nods in air;
Eternal winds Keen, hollow winds howl thro' the bleak recess, *intell*
20 Emblem of music caus'd by emptiness:
Here in one bed two shiv'ring sisters lye,
The cave of *Poverty* and *Poetry*.
This, the *Great Mother* dearer held than all
The clubs of *Quidnunc's*, or her own *Guild-hall*:
kept 25 Here stood her Opium, here she nurs'd her Owls,
And destin'd here th' imperial seat of fools.
Hence springs each weekly muse, the living boast
Of C——l's chaste press, and L——t's rubric post; *into*

v. 17. *There yawns a Ruin pervious to ye Air,* Hence
Some say in Kentstreet, others in Rag-Fair.

Book the First.

Hence hymning *Tyburn*'s elegiac lay,
30 Hence the soft sing-song on *Cecilia*'s day,
Sepulchral lyes our holy walls to grace,
And *New-year-Odes*, and all the *Grubstreet* race.

'Twas here in clouded majesty she shone;
Four guardian *Virtues*, round, support her throne;
35 Fierce champion *Fortitude*, that knows no fears
Of hisses, blows, or want, or loss of ears:
Calm *Temperance*, whose blessings those partake
Who hunger, and who thirst for scribling sake:
Prudence, whose glass presents th' approaching jayl;
40 Poetic *Justice*, with her lifted scale;
Where in nice balance, truth with gold she weighs,
And solid pudding against empty praise.

Here she beholds the Chaos dark and deep,
Where nameless *somethings* in their causes sleep,
45 'Till genial *Jacob*, or a warm *third-day*
Calls forth each mass, a poem or a play.
How hints, like spawn, scarce quick in embryo lie;
How new-born nonsense first is taught to cry;

The DUNCIAD.

Maggots half-form'd, in rhyme exactly meet,
50 And learn to crawl upon poetic feet.
Here one poor *Word* a hundred clenches makes,
And ductile dulness new meanders takes;
There motley *Images* her fancy strike,
Figures ill-pair'd, and *Similes* unlike.
55 She sees a mob of *Metaphors* advance,
Pleas'd with the madness of the mazy dance;
How *Tragedy* and *Comedy* embrace;
How *Farce* and *Epic* get a jumbled race;
How *Time* himself stands still at her command,
60 Realms shift their place, and Ocean turns to land.
Here gay *Description* Ægypt glads with showers,
Or gives to *Zembla* fruits, to *Barca* flowers;
Glitt'ring with ice here hoary hills are seen,
Fast by, fair vallies of eternal green,
65 On cold *December* fragrant chaplets blow,
And heavy harvests nod beneath the snow.

All these and more, the cloud-compelling Queen
Beholds thro' fogs, that magnify the scene;

Marginal annotations:

Now
And two-shap'd Tropes (joyn'd 2
Now sees contending
th'unmeasur'd 1
Now
Now

Her unconfin'd Descr. paints

There smiling
flowry

int.

aft. v. 52 Here Atom Swarms of thin conceits unwrought, She
There Hints like Spawn slow quickning into Thought.

aft. v. 58. On Summer's neck his Arms here Autumn flings,
And naked Winters marry blooming Springs.

BOOK the FIRST.

[margin: Refulgent] She, tinsel'd o'er in robes of varying hues, *[margin: She high enthron'd]*
70 With self-applause her wild creation views,
Sees momentary monsters rise and fall,
And with her own fools-colours gilds them all. *[margin: 'Twas — But here a leaf]*
[margin: & Ettere of whole speech — v. 217.   Torn out to v. 225.]

'Twas on the day, when † Tho——d, rich and grave,
Like ‡ Cimon triumph'd both on land and wave,
75 (Pomps without guilt, of bloodless swords and maces,
Glad chains, warm furs, broad banners, and broad faces)
Now night descending, the proud scene was o'er,
Yet liv'd, in Settle's numbers, one day more.
Now May'rs and Shrieves in pleasing slumbers lay,
80 And eat in dreams the custard of the day;
But pensive poets painful vigils keep;
Sleepless themselves, to give their readers sleep.
Much to her mind the solemn feast recalls,
What city-Swans once sung within the walls.
85 Much she revolves their arts, their antient praise,
And sure succession down from * Heywood's days.

† Sir Geo. Tho—— ‡ Cimon the famous Athenian general, who obtained a victory by sea, and another by land, on the same day, over the Persians and Barbarians. * John Heywood, whose Interludes were printed in Hen. VIIIth's time.

B 3

The DUNCIAD.

She saw with joy the line immortal run,
Each fire imprest and glaring in his son;
So watchful *Bruin* forms with plastic care
90 Each growing lump, and brings it to a Bear.
She saw in N——n all his father shine,
And E——n eke out Bl——'s endless line;
She saw flow P——s creep like T——te's poor page,
And furious D——n foam in Wh——'s rage.

95   In each, she marks her image full exprest,
But chief, in *Tibbald*'s monster-breeding breast,
Sees Gods with Dæmons in strange league ingage,
And † earth, and heav'n, and hell, her battels wage!

She ey'd the Bard where supperless he sate,
100 And pin'd, unconscious of his rising fate;
Studious he sate, with all his books around,
Sinking from thought to thought, a vast profound!
Plung'd for his sense, but found no bottom there:
Then writ, and flounder'd on, in mere despair.

† This, I presume, alludes to the extravagancies of the Farces of this author. See book III. vers. 170, &c.

He

Book the First.

105 He roll'd his eyes that witness'd huge dismay,
Where yet unpawn'd, much learned lumber lay,
Volumes, whose size the space exactly fill'd;
Or which fond authors were so good to gild;
Or where, by Sculpture made for ever known,
110 The page admires new beauties, not its own.
Here swells the shelf with *Ogleby* the *great*,
There, stamp'd with arms, *Newcastle* shines compleat,
Here all his suff'ring brotherhood retire,
And 'scape the martyrdom of jakes and fire;
115 A *Gothic* Vatican! of *Greece* and *Rome*
Well-purg'd, and worthy W——, W——s, and Bl——
But high above, more solid Learning shone,
The *Classicks* of an age that heard of none;
There *Caxton* slept, with *Wynkin* at his side,
120 One clasp'd in wood, and one in strong cow-hide:
There sav'd by spice, like mummies, many a year,
Old Bodies of Philosophy appear:
De Lyra there a dreadful front extends,
And there, the groaning Shelves *Philemon* bends.

125 Of these twelve volumes, twelve of amplest size,
Redeem'd from tapers and defrauded pyes,
Inspir'd he seizes: These an altar raise:
An hecatomb of pure, unsully'd lays
That altar crowns; a folio Common-place
130 Founds the whole pyle, of all his works the base:
Quarto's, octavo's, shape the lessening pyre,
And last, a † *little Ajax* tips the spire.

Then he. Great Tamer of all human art!
First in my care, and nearest at my heart!
135 *Dulness!* whose good old cause I yet defend,
With whom my muse began, with whom shall end;
Oh thou! of business the directing soul,
To human heads like byass to the bowl,
Which as more pond'rous makes their aim more true,
140 Obliquely wadling to the mark in view.
O ever gracious to perplex'd mankind!
Who spread a healing mist before the mind,
And, lest we err by wit's wild, dancing light,
Secure us kindly in our native *night*.

† In duodecimo, translated from *Sophocles*.

Book the FIRST:

145 Ah! still o'er *Britain* stretch that peaceful wand,
   Which lulls th' *Helvetian* and *Batavian* land,
   Where 'gainst thy throne if rebel Science rise,
   She does but show her coward face and dies:
   There, thy good *scholiasts* with unweary'd pains
150 Make *Horace* flat, and humble *Maro*'s strains;
   Here studious I unlucky Moderns save,
   Nor sleeps one error in its father's grave,
   Old puns restore, lost blunders nicely seek,
   And crucify poor *Shakespear* once a week.
155 For thee I dim these eyes, and stuff this head,
   With all such reading as was never read;
   For thee supplying, in the worst of days,
   Notes to dull books, and Prologues to dull plays;
   For thee explain a thing 'till all men doubt it,
160 And write about it, Goddess, and about it;
   So spins the silkworm small its slender store,
   And labours, 'till it clouds itself all o'er.
   Not that my pen to criticks was confin'd,
   My verse gave ampler lessons to mankind;
165 So written precepts may successless prove,
   But sad examples never fail to move.

The DUNCIAD.

As forc'd from wind-guns, lead itself can fly,
And pond'rous slugs cut swiftly thro' the sky;
As clocks to weight their nimble motion owe,
170 The wheels above urg'd by the load below;
Me, Emptiness and Dulness could inspire,
And were my Elasticity, and Fire.
Had heav'n decreed such works a longer date,
Heav'n had decreed to spare the *Grubstreet*-state.
175 But see * great *Settle* to the dust descend,
And all thy cause and empire at an end!
Cou'd *Troy* be sav'd by any single hand,
His gray-goose-weapon must have made her stand.
But what can I! my *Flaccus* cast aside,
180 Take up th' *Attorney's* (once my better) guide?
Or rob the *Roman* geese of all their glories,
And save the state by cackling to the Tories?
Yes, to my country I my pen consign,
Yes, from this moment, mighty *Mist!* am thine,

* This was the last year of *Elkanah Settle*'s life. He was poet to the city of *London*, whose business was to compose yearly panegyricks on the Lord Mayor, and verses for the Pageants; but since the abolition of that part of the shows, the employment ceas'd, so that *Settle* had no successor to that place.

And

Book the First. 11

185 And rival, *Curtius!* of thy fame and zeal,
O'er head and ears plunge for the public weal.
Adieu my children! better thus expire
Un-stall'd, unfold; thus glorious mount in fire
Fair without spot; than greas'd by grocer's hands,
190 Or shipp'd with W——d to ape and monkey lands,
Or wafting ginger, round the streets to go,
And visit alehouse where ye first did grow.

With that, he lifted thrice the sparkling brand,
And thrice he dropt it from his quiv'ring hand:
195 Then lights the structure, with averted eyes;
The rowling smokes involve the sacrifice.
The opening clouds disclose each work by turns,
Now flames old * *Memnon,* now *Rodrigo* burns,
In one quick flash see *Proserpine* expire,
200 And last, his own cold *Æschylus* took fire.
Then gush'd the tears, as from the *Trojan's* eyes
When the last blaze sent *Ilion* to the skies.

* Plays and Farces of T——d.

C 2   Rowz'd

The DUNCIAD.

Rowz'd by the light, old *Dulness* heav'd the head,
Then snatch'd a sheet of *Thule* from her Bed,
205 Sudden she flies, and whelms it o'er the pyre;
Down sink the flames, and with a hiss expire.

Her ample presence fills up all the place;
A veil of fogs dilates her awful face,
Great in her charms! as when on Shrieves and May'rs
210 She looks, and breathes herself into their airs.
She bids him wait her to the sacred Dome;
Well-pleas'd he enter'd, and confess'd his home:
So spirits, ending their terrestrial race,
Ascend, and recognize their native place;
215 Raptur'd, he gazes round the dear retreat,
And ‡ in sweet numbers celebrates the seat.

See att. v. 72. Here to her Chosen all her works she shows;
Prose swell'd to verse, Verse loitring into prose:
How random thoughts now meaning chance to find,
220 Now leave all memory of sense behind:

‡ He writ a poem called the *Cave of Poverty*, printed in 1715.

How Unideal thoughts now meaning find,
Now leave —— to ozell.

BOOK the FIRST. 13

How Prologues into Prefaces decay,
And those to Notes are fritter'd quite away:
How Index-learning turns no student pale,
Yet holds the eel of science by the Tail:
225 How, with less reading than makes felons 'scape,
Less human genius than God gives an ape,
Small thanks to *France*, and none to *Rome* or *Greece*,
A past, vamp'd, future, old, reviv'd, new piece,
'Twixt *Plautus, Fletcher, Congreve,* and *Corneille,*
230 Can make a C——r, Jo——n, or O——ll.

The Goddess then, o'er his anointed head,
With mystic words the sacred Opium shed;
And lo! her *Bird* (a monster of a fowl!
Something betwixt a H—— and Owl)
235 Perch'd on his crown. All hail! and hail again
My son! the promis'd land expects thy reign.
Know *Settle,* cloy'd with custard and with praise,
Is gather'd to the Dull of antient days,
Safe, where no criticks damn, no duns molest,
240 Where G——n, B——, and high-born H—— rest!

14 The DUNCIAD.

I see a King! who leads my chosen sons
To lands that flow with clenches and with puns:
'Till each fam'd theatre my empire own,
Till *Albion*, as *Hibernia*, bless my throne.
245 I see! I see!—Then rapt, she spoke no more.
God save King Tibbald! *Grubstreet* alleys roar.

So when *Jove*'s block descended from on high,
(As sings thy great fore-father, *Ogilby*,)
Hoarse thunder to its bottom shook the bog,
250 And the loud nation croak'd, *God save King Log*!

End of the first Book.

Marginalia (left):
g—save King T—
Take thou y Sceptre, rule
realms
And till both Theatres
And near our Monarchs Duck

shook y bottom of

Marginalia (bottom):
aft v. 242. God save King T— Grubstreet own our C͞h͞i͞e͞f
And Hawkers Heralds roar with rusty voice.

THE DUNCIAD.

Book the Second.

HE sons of *Dulness* meet: an endless band [*She summons all her Sons;*]
Pours forth, and leaves unpeopled half the land, [*dispeopled*]
A motley mixture! in long wigs, in bags, [*of*]
In silks, in crapes, in garters, and in rags;
5 From drawing rooms, from colleges, from garrets,
On horse, on foot, in hacks, and gilded chariots,
All who true Dunces in her cause appear'd,
And all who knew those Dunces to reward.

Now

The DUNCIAD.

                                            to grace the day
                           The Goddess now by Hawker's voice
To these ye Queen by Trumpets sound Now herald hawker's rusty voice proclaims
                        10 Heroic prizes, and advent'rous Games;   with authors v. 15
Amid that Area wide she   In that wide space the Goddess took her stand
                            Where the tall May-pole once o'erlook'd the Strand;
                            But now (so ANNE and Piety ordain)
        invites   A Church collects the saints of Drury-lane.
                               with authors Stationers — The field &c.
                               Ev'n Booksellers obey ye Hawker's call;   all
   Booksellers   15 With authors, stationers obey'd the call;   To these in short the first prophet
                            The field of glory is a field for all; who sit &c.   that such as &c. — v. 21.
                            Glory, and gain, th' industrious tribe provoke,
                            And gentle Dulness ever loves a joke.
                            A Poet's Form she sets before their eyes,
                        20 And bids the nimblest racer seize the prize;
Not such as Garrets lodge of   where
                            No meagre, muse-rid mope, adust and thin,
Who like a N-g- round him wraps his In a dun night-gown of his own loose skin;
                            But such a bulk as no twelve bards could raise,
       starveling   Twelve starving bards of these degen'rate days. qualis qui
plump as a P- ruddy, round 25 All as a partridge plump, full-fed, and fair, Rem — forditi
                              * She form'd this image of well-bodied air, *Tumidea nil
Laugh'd eyes ye twinkled in his With pert flat eyes she window'd well its head,
Well-look'd, well-trussed, well A brain of feathers, and a heart of lead, a turd, & well fed,
So wondrous like that Wootton's self Mr. Tay, Aug Kent w. sweas, by S— d   And before
 All gaze v. 35
                            Who sit at Counters or at Rails who stand,
                        ]. From Pauls, Moorfields, Pye corner, or ye Strand;
    impudent   And last in infamous Disorder came
   * . Pyrates, & Publishers, unknown to fame.
                           In Fleetsheet fair the Goddess chose ye place,
  Then   And mark'd the Barriers, & prescrib'd the Race.
                           And first (for Dullness, gentle Queen! delights
                           In Jokes, & feeds her Subjects with strange sights)
                           To nimble Stationers propos'd the Prize;
mark'd a Poet's Phant And sets a Phantome Poet in their eyes.
  * Multos praeterea quos fama obscura recondit.   Not such v. 21

BOOK the SECOND. 17

And empty words she gave, and sounding strain;
30 But senseless, lifeless! Idol void and vain!
Never was dasht out, at one lucky hit,
A fool, so just a copy of a wit;
So like, that criticks said and courtiers swore,
A wit it was, and call'd the phantom, M—.

35 All gaze with ardour: some, a Poet's name, *the Author's fame,*
Others, a sword-knot and lac'd suit inflame: *his lace, & Birthday*
But lofty L—*[into]* in the circle rose; *awfull Tryphon*
" This prize is mine; who tempt it, are my foes:
" With me began this genius, and shall end:
40 He spoke, and who with L—*[Tonson]* shall contend? *Tryphon*

Fear held them mute. Alone, untaught to fear,
Stood dauntless C—l. " Behold that rival here! *your*
" The race by vigor, not by vaunts is won;
" So take the hindmost Hell.—He said, and run.
45 Swift as a bard the bailiff leaves behind, *his*
He left huge L—t, and out-stript the wind. *fat Tonson / Tryphon /*
As when a dab-chick waddles thro' the copse,
On legs and wings, and flies, and wades, and hops;

D So

18   The DUNCIAD.

So lab'ring on, with shoulders, hands, and head, *arms*
50 Wide as a windmill all his figure spread, *Tryphon w. Arms expanded shows his State / Tonson*
With steps unequal L—t urg'd the race, *his Uncle*
And seem'd to emulate great *Jacob*'s pace. *And left-legg'd Jacob seems to emulate* | *so first*
Full in the middle way there stood a lake,
Which C—l's *Corinna* chanc'd that morn to make, *...Harlot happ'd*
55 (Such was her wont, at early dawn to drop
Her evening cates before his neighbour's shop,)
Here fortun'd C—l to slide: loud shout the band, *shudder'd Curl   Laugh'd*
And L—t, L—t, rings thro' all the *Strand*. *Tryphon moves ye Glory of / flies / Jacob, Jacob*
Obscene with filth the varlet lies betray'd,
60 Fal'n in the plash his wickedness had lay'd:
Then first (if Poets ought of truth declare)
The caitiff *Vaticide* conceiv'd a prayer.

Hear *Jove!* whose name my bards and I adore,
As much at least as any Gods, or more;
And him and his, if more devotion warms, *Vand if in Him & His more / In him this if greater Grace above*
Down with the * *Bible*, up with the † *Pope's Arms*. *Then let mine Host of Skys wth he crown'd / d. If He & His more pious trim ye Scales, Then let mine Host of Skys h prevail.*

* The Bible C——'s sign.   † The Cross-keys L——t's. *x Head of Shakspears head / Tonsons sign*

v. 65. *In Him if His unless more Grace appear, / This Days bright Garland let not Tryphon wear* / *wreath of Conquest* A
Brown Cloacina heard her Servant call, / From her black Grottos near ye Temple Wall / A place —

v. 52 *Sequiturq patrem non passibus æquis.*
v. 54 *One Mrs Thomas who call'd her self K——*

Book the Second. 19

‡ A place there is, betwixt earth, air and seas, *between*
Where from *Ambrosia*, *Jove* retires for ease. *Call'd ---*
There in his seat two spacious Vents appear, *throne*
70 On this he sits, to that he leans his ear, *this*
There hears the various vows of fond mankind,
Some beg an eastern, some a western wind:
All vain petitions, sent by winds on high, *Petitions vain ye daily vex ye Sky,*
With reams abundant this abode supply;
75 Amus'd he reads, and then returns the bills *Jove reads them ov^r & is those usefull*
Sign'd with that *Ichor* which from Gods distills. *Wipes that rich then gath'ring all y^e*

In office here fair *Cloacina* stands, *black*
And ministers to *Jove* with purest hands;
Forth from the heap she pick'd her vot'ry's pray'r,
80 And plac'd it next him, a distinction rare! *foremost*
Oft, as he fish'd her nether realms for wit,
The Goddess favour'd him, and favours yet. *this*
Renew'd by ordure's sympathetic force,
As oil'd with magic juices for the course,
85 Vig'rous he rises; from th' effluvia strong
Imbibes new life, and scours and stinks along,

‡ See *Lucian's Icaro-Menippus.*

v. 67. A Place there is between earth, Air, & Seas,
Call'd by the Gods the Thunderer's House of Ease.
Where in her Throne two Spacious vents appear,
On one she sits, to one applys her Ear:
There lists delighted to ye Jest unclean
Of Link-boys vile, & watermen obscene.
Then with Mist's Journals, & with Tanner's Bills
 Goddess
Wipes that rich Ichor which a God distills.
Oft as she fish'd these nether ——— v. 81.

Cloacina. Gay's Trivia 15? quote ——

20   The DUNCIAD.
     Re-passes L—t, vindicates the race,
     Nor heeds the brown dishonours of his face.

        And now the victor stretch'd his eager hand,
90   Where the tall Nothing stood, or seem'd to stand;
     A shapeless shade, it melted from his sight,
     Like forms in clouds, or visions of the night!
     Baffled, yet present ev'n amidst despair,
     To seize his papers, C—l, was next thy care;
95   His papers all, the sportive winds up-lift,
     And whisk 'em back to G—, to Y—, to S—.
     Th' embroider'd suit, at least, he deem'd his prey;
     That suit, an unpay'd Taylor snatch'd away!
     No rag, no scrap, of all the beau, or wit,
100 That once so flutter'd, and that once so writ.

        Heav'n rings with laughter: Of the laughter vain,
     Dulness, good Queen, repeats the jest again.
     Three wicked imps of her own Grubstreet Choir
     She deck'd like Congreve, Addison, and Prior;
105 Mears, Warner, Wilkins run: Delusive thought!
     **, **, and **, the wretches caught.
                                                C—l

BOOK the SECOND. 21

C—l stretches after *Gay*, but *Gay* is gone,
He grasps an empty † *Joseph* for a *John*.
So *Proteus*, hunted in a nobler shape,
110 Became, when seiz'd, a Puppy or an Ape.

To him the Goddess. Son, thy grief lay down,
And turn this whole illusion on the town.
As the sage dame experienc'd in her trade,
By names of Toasts retails each batter'd jade,
115 (Whence hapless Monsieur much complains at *Paris*
Of wrongs from Duchesses and Lady *Marys*)
Be thine, my stationer! this magic gift;
C— shall be *Prior*, and C—n, *Swift*;
So shall each hostile name become our own,
120 And we too boast our *Garth* and *Addison*.

With that the Goddess (piteous of his case,
Yet smiling at his ruful length of face)
Gives him a cov'ring, worthy to be spread
On *Codrus'* old, or * * 's modern bed;

† *Joseph Gay*, a fictitious name put by C——l before several
Pamphlets.

Instructive

Handwritten annotations:

Pleas'd at her Wit, & of applauses vain,
Dullness, good Queen, repeats the Jest again.
Another Poet, & another rise,
Curl, not discourag'd, at each quarry flies.
Forthwith he drest, like Addison & Prior,
Two Wicked Imps of her own Grubstreet Quire.
A Wicked Spright she drest in Pope's attire.
The same the voice, the mein, & the attire.

[N. a Leaf torn out to v. 172.]

125 Instructive work! whose wry-mouth'd portraiture
Display'd the fates her confessors endure.
Ear-less on high, stood pillory'd D——foe
And T—— flagrant from the lash, below:
There kick'd and cudgel'd R— might ye view,
The very worstead still look'd black and blue:
130 Himself among the storied chiefs he spies,
As from the blanket high in air he flies;
And oh! (he cry'd) what street, what lane but knows
Our purgings, pumpings, blanketings and blows?
In ev'ry loom our labors shall be seen,
135 And the fresh vomit run for ever green!

See in the circle next, *Eliza* plac'd;
Two babes of love close clinging to her waste;
Fair as before her works she stands confess'd,
In flow'r'd brocade by bounteous *Kirkall* dress'd,
140 Pearls on her neck, and roses in her hair,
And her fore-buttocks to the navel bare.
The Goddess then: "Who best can send on high
"The salient spout, fair-streaming to the sky;

"His

Book the Second.   23

"His! be yon *Juno* of majestic size,
145 "With cow-like udders, and with ox-like eyes.
"This *China*-Jordan, let the chief o'ercome
"Replenish; not ingloriously, at home.

C——d and C——l accept this glorious strife, *(Chetwood & Curl)*
(Tho' one his Son dissuades, and one his Wife)
150 This on his manly confidence relies,
That on his vigor and superior size.

First C——d lean'd against his letter'd post;
It rose, and labor'd to a curve at most:
So *Jove*'s bright bow displays its watry round,
155 (Sure sign, that no spectator shall be drown'd)
A second effort brought but new disgrace,
For straining more, it flies in his own face;
Thus the small jett which hasty hands unlock,
Spirits in the gard'ners eyes who turns the cock.
160 Not so from shameless C——l: Impetuous spread
The stream, and smoaking, flourish'd o'er his head.
So, (fam'd like thee for turbulence and horns,)
Eridanus his humble fountain scorns.

Thro'

24   The DUNCIAD.
        Thro' half the heav'ns he pours th' exalted urn;
165 His rapid waters in their passage burn.

        Swift as it mounts, all follow with their eyes;
        Still happy, Impudence obtains the prize.
        Thou triumph'st, Victor of the high-wrought day,
        And the pleas'd dame soft-smiling leads away.
170 Ch——d, through perfect modesty o'ercome,
        Crown'd with the Jordan, walks contented home.

        But now for *Authors* nobler palms remain:
        Room for my Lord! three Jockeys in his train;
        Six huntsmen with a shout precede his chair;
175 He grins, and looks broad nonsense with a stare.
        His honour'd meaning, *Dulness* thus exprest.
        "He wins this Patron who can tickle best."

        He chinks his purse, and takes his seat of state,
        With ready quills the Dedicators wait,
180 Now at his head the dext'rous task commence,
        And instant, fancy feels th' imputed sense;
                                                        Now

BOOK the SECOND. 23

  Now gentle touches wanton o'er his face,
3 { He struts *Adonis*, and affects grimace:
  R—— the feather to his ear conveys,
        all
185 Then his nice taste directs our *Operas*:   *He turns Subscriber to all*
    B——y
int { ** his mouth with *Classic* flatt'ry opes,
  And the puft *Orator* bursts out in tropes.   *breaks*
while { But O—— *Oldmixon* the *Poet's* healing balm
  Strives to extract from his soft, giving palm:
190 Unlucky O——! thy lordly master   *Unhappy*   *Lord &*
  The more thou ticklest, gripes his fist the faster.

  While thus each hand promotes the pleasing pain,
  And quick sensations skip from vein to vein,
  A youth unknown to *Phœbus*, in despair,
195 Puts his last refuge all in Heav'n in Pray'r.
  What force have pious vows? the *Queen* of *Love*
  His Sister sends, her vot'ress, from above.
  As taught by *Venus, Paris* learnt the art   *So, Great Achilles!*
        from it
  To touch *Achilles'* only tender part,   *thy only penetrable*
200 Secure, thro' her, the noble prize to carry,   *By Venus taught*
  He marches off, his Grace's *Secretary*.

---

aft. v. 183.   H   E   Now
Now, to his Heart ye Titillation comes,
this beating bosom pants
He pants with Courage, & wth love of Drums:
  Bentley *wth Bentley's Classic flatt'ry*
His Mouth now Bentley's kind Instruction opes,
    bawls / roars
He grows an Orator, & out fly Tropes.

v. 188. Concanen, from his Soft & Giving Palm,
Strives to extract ye Poet's healing Balm.
Unhappy Concanen! ——— *faster.*

A Nicer part sly W——t chose to probe,
     Zahass
Latent beneath ye Cincture of his Robe
Where ... *azure cincture says'd to hold* ... *distinct wth varied gold.*
his well observ'd, unheeded by the rest,
He brought his Sister, & she tickled best.
So Great Achilles

aft. v. 202 The Head who wins not may y'e Ear confound,
And force Attention, not by Sense, but Sound.

The Last, not wholly to Lament his fate,
A Groat to Drink, or ——————'s Works compleat.

26 The DUNCIAD.

                     other
Now turn to diff'rent sports (the Goddess cries)
And learn, my sons, the wond'rous pow'r of *Noise*.
To move, to raise, to ravish ev'ry heart,
With *Shakespear*'s nature, or with *Johnson*'s art,
205 Let others aim: 'Tis yours to shake the soul
       By   *rattling*
With *Thunder* rumbling from the mustard-bowl,
                   fury
With *horns* and *trumpets* now to madness swell,
Now sink in sorrows with a tolling *Bell*,
   These
Such happy arts attention can command,
   The
210 When fancy flags, and sense is at a stand:
Improve we these. Three *Cat-calls* be the bribe
Of him, whose chatt'ring shames the *Monkey* tribe;
   But
And his this *Drum*, whose hoarse heroic base
Drowns the loud Clarion of the braying *Ass*.

[*See Reverse of ye title Page.*]
                   Criticks all rush
215 Now thousand tongues are heard in one loud din,
The Monkey-mimicks rush discordant in;
'Twas chatt'ring, grinning, mouthing, jabb'ring all,
         Welsh'd at Wicksted, Budge'd at Brevel,
And R—o—e, and railing, Brangling, and B——,
                  and loud tongu'd
& each sustains his part D——s and Dissonance; And captious art,
with
220 And snip-snap short, and interruption smart.

Hold for Noise & Nonsense next behold y'e Prize,
Whose Voice Stentonian louder shakes y'e Skies.
Who fails to ravish, or command y'e Heart,
With Shakears Nature, or with Johnsons art,
Shall wake y'e Sense, & ravishe y'e Soul,
                    ac
With rolling thunders from y'e Mustard-Bowl.
    move
{ Move dullest minds, from Passion quite at ease,
{ With Show'rs of Paper, or by Hail of Pease.
                  now to Vengeance
With Horns, & trumpets each tho —— to swell
now *in*
Or sink in Sorrow with a tolling Bell.
From Pathos, & from Ethos quite at ease,
Alarm an Audience with a Storm of Pease.

                                Theb. Mary.

BOOK the SECOND.   27

Hold (cry'd the Queen) ye all alike shall win,
Equal your merits, equal is your din:
But that this well-disputed game may end,
Sound forth my *Brayers*, and the welkin rend.

225 As when the long-ear'd, milky mothers wait
At some sick miser's triple-bolted gate,
For their defrauded, absent foals they make
A moan so loud, that all the *Guild* awake:
So sighs Sir G———t, starting at the bray

230 From dreams of millions, and three groats to pay.
So swells each Windpipe; Ass intones to Ass,
Harmonic twang! of leather, horn, and brass:
Such as from lab'ring lungs th' Enthusiast blows,
High sounds, attempted to the vocal nose.

235 But far o'er all sonorous Bl——'s strain,
Walls, steeples, skies, bray back to him again:
In *Tot'nham* fields, the brethren with amaze
Prick all their ears up, and forget to graze;
Long *Chanc'ry-lane* retentive rolls the sound,

240 And courts to courts return it round and round:

28   The DUNCIAD.

Thames wafts it thence to *Rufus*' roaring hall,
And H———d re-ecchoes, bawl for bawl.
All hail him victor in both gifts of Song,
Who sings so *loudly*, and who sings so *long*.

245 This labor past, by *Bridewell* all descend,
    (As morning pray'r and flagellation end.)
    To where *Fleetditch* with disemboguing streams
    Rolls the large tribute of dead dogs to *Thames*,
    The King of Dykes! than whom, no sluice of mud
250 With deeper sable blots the silver flood.
    ' Here strip my children! here at once leap in!
    ' Here prove who best can dash thro' thick and thin,
    ' And who the most in love of dirt excel,
    ' Or dark dexterity of groping well.
255 ' Who flings most mud, and wide pollutes around
    ' The stream, be his the ✱ ✱ ✱ *Journals*, bound.
    ' A pig of lead to him who dives the best;
    ' A peck of coals a-piece shall glad the rest.

    In naked majesty great D——— stands,
260 And, *Milo*-like, surveys his arms and hands:

                                          Then

[margin notes: Hungerford— ; This game is wholly torn out, from the preced verse — so long, to v. 317, slow mov'd ; weekly ; Dennis]

Book the Second.   29

Then sighing, thus. " And am I now *threescore?*
" Ah why, ye Gods! should two and two make four?
He said, and climb'd a stranded Lighter's height,
Shot to the black abyss, and plung'd down-right.
265 The senior's judgment all the crowd admire,
Who but to sink the deeper, rose the higher.

Next E— div'd; slow circles dimpled o'er
The quaking mud, that clos'd and ope'd no more:
All look, all sigh, and call on E— lost;
270 E—— in vain resounds thro' all the coast.

H— try'd the next, but hardly snatch'd from sight,
Instant buoys up, and rises into light;
He bears no token of the sabler streams,
And mounts far off, among the swans of *Thames.*

275 Far worse unhappy D——t succeeds,
He search'd for coral, but he gather'd weeds.

True to the bottom, *** and *** creep,
Long-winded both, as natives of the deep,

This

30   The DUNCIAD.

This only merit pleading for the prize,
280 Nor everlasting *Bl——* this denies.

[Welstead]

But nimbler W——d reaches at the ground,
Circles in mud, and darkness all around,
No crab more active, in the dirty dance,
Downward to climb, and backward to advance;
285 He brings up half the bottom on his head,
And boldly claims the *Journals* and the *Lead.*

Sudden, a burst of thunder shook the flood,

[Eusden—]

Lo E—— rose, tremendous all in mud!
Shaking the horrors of his sable brows,
290 And each ferocious feature grim with ooze.
Greater he looks, and more than mortal stares;
Then thus the wonders of the deep declares.

First he relates, how sinking to the chin,
Smit with his mien, the *Mudnymphs* suck'd him in,
295 How young *Lutetia* softer than the down,
Nigrina black, and *Merdamante* brown,

Vy'd

Book the Second.

Vy'd for his love in jetty bow'rs below;
As *Hylas* fair was ravish'd long ago.
Then sung how, shown him by the nutbrown maids
300 A branch of *Styx* here rises from the *Shades*,
That tinctur'd as it runs with *Lethe*'s streams,
And wafting vapors from the *Land* of *Dreams*,
(As under seas *Alphæus* sacred sluice
Bears *Pisa*'s offerings to his *Arethuse*)
305 Pours into *Thames*: Each City-bowl is full
Of the mixt wave, and all who drink grow dull.
How, to the banks where bards departed doze,
They led him soft; how all the bards arose;
Taylor, sweet bird of *Thames*, majestic bows,
310 And *Sh—* nods the poppy on his brows;
While *M—n* there, deputed by the rest,
Gave him the cassock, surcingle, and vest;
And "Take (he said) these robes which once were
" Dulness is sacred in a sound Divine. (mine,

315 He ceas'd, and show'd the robe; the crowd confess
The rev'rend *Flamen* in his lengthen'd dress.

Slow

32   The DUNCIAD.

Slow mov'd the Goddess from the silver flood,
(Her Priest preceding) thro' the gates of *Lud*.
Her *Criticks* there she summons, and proclaims
320 A gentler exercise to close the games.

Hear you! in whose grave heads, as equal scales,
I weigh what author's heaviness prevails,
Which most conduce to sooth the soul in slumbers,
My H——'s periods, or my Bl——'s numbers?
325 Attend the trial we propose to make:
If there be man who o'er such works can wake,
Sleep's all-subduing pow'r who dares defy,
And boasts *Ulysses*' ear with *Argus*' eye;
To him we grant our amplest pow'rs to sit
330 Judge of all present, past, and future wit,
To cavil, censure, dictate, right or wrong,
Full, and eternal privilege of tongue.

Three *Cambridge Sophs* and three pert *Templars* came,
The same their talents, and their tastes the same;
                                                    Each

Marginal annotations (manuscript):

[See ad v. 245.]

My Critics in whose
bless Mank-w-d-th   Henley's
Is now the

Him we invest with

critic
and his th'

v. 30. This done, the Goddess, from the sable flood,
Moves to her quarters in the Walls of Lud; Gates
The Tribes persue; And now to close the Games,
A gentler Exercise the Queen proclaims.
Her Priest attends: In honor of whose
She calls her Critics now to close ye Games. Hear you

aft v. 328. His be the our Licence, which shall ever last,
On all my authors, present, future, past.
To critic —   and his Eternal
nemo   Yet not to plunge Well-Willers in Dispair,
emo in hoc nu: Who hapy Slumbers shall some Reward share.
um mihi non   To Him who nodding sleeps a transient nap,
natus abilit.   We give Tate's Ovid, & thy Virgil, Trap,
                     Unable Heads that sleep & wake by fits,
                     Win steel, well-sifted from all alien Wits.
                     Nay was Successless quite but only 99 — & wish,
                     Shall gain the whole Poetic Art of By, She — Three Camb-

Book the Second.

335 Each prompt to query, answer, and debate,
And smit with love of poesie and prate.
The pond'rous books two *gentle Readers* bring;
The heroes sit; the vulgar form a ring.
The clam'rous crowd is hush'd with mugs of *Mum*,
340 'Till all tun'd equal, send a general hum.
Then mount the Clerks; and in one lazy tone,
Thro' the long, heavy, painful page, drawl on,
Soft creeping words on words the sense compose,
At e'vry line, they stretch, they yawn, they doze.
345 As to soft gales top-heavy pines bow low
Their heads, and lift them as they cease to blow,
Thus oft they rear, and oft the head decline,
As breathe, or pause, by fits, the airs divine.
And now to this side, now to that, they nod,
350 As verse, or prose, infuse the drowzy God.
Thrice B——l aim'd to speak, but thrice supprest
By potent *Arthur*, knock'd his chin and breast.
C——s and T——d, prompt at Priests to jeer,
Yet silent bow'd to *Christ's-no-kingdom* here.
355 Who sate the nearest, by the word's o'ercome
Slept first, the distant nodded to the hum.

Then

34   The DUNCIAD.

Then down are roll'd the books; stretch'd o'er 'em lies
Each gentle clerk, and mutt'ring seals his eyes.
As what a *Dutchman* plumps into the lakes,
360 One circle first, and then a second makes,
What dulness dropt among her sons imprest
Like motion, from one circle to the rest;
So from the mid-most the nutation spreads
Round, and more round, o'er all the sea of heads.
365 At last C——re felt her voice to fail,
And *** himself unfinish'd left his Tale.
T——s and T——p the church and state gave o'er,
Nor *** talk'd, nor S———— whisper'd more.
Ev'n N————n, gifted with his mother's tongue,
370 Tho' born at *Wapping*, and from *Daniel* sprung,
Ceas'd his loud bawling breath, and dropt the head;
And all was hush'd, as *Folly*'s self lay dead.

Thus the soft gifts of *Sleep* conclude the day,
And stretch'd on bulks, as usual, Poets lay.
375 Why should I sing what bards the Nightly Muse
Did slumbring visit, and convey to stews?

[marginal annotations and manuscript revisions:]

fall'n
add
a lake
Will first one Circle, then a —— makes
amid
Catch'd by   first, the nodding
    fell
length Centlivre —
Bruce
              forgot
Kelsal   Laughton
..tho fam'd for foul debate
Sprung from Defoe & born at Billingsgate
Ev'n He sate mute on Critic's Criticks spread

Bards around on Bulks, as usual
Except whom in he walks
[Here MS torn off]

[aft. v.364] Not more when winds succeed some heavy Rain, Or
Unnumber'd nod the Poppies of the Plain.
δ] The Clerks themselves dropt down on either side
Down roll the Volumes, o'er each Volume lies
The gentle Clerk, & muttring shuts his Eyes.
Then first Centlivre —

v. 367. Travers & Trap, untir'd in long debate,
One for the Church, the other for the State;
∂   Frazer, who talk'd ten Volumes o'er by heart,
And Boyer gifted with his Mothers art,
Lay Mute, All slept, ev'n Norton calm in Silence slept,
Sprung from Defoe, & born at Bilingsgate:
Wits roll'd on wits, on Critics Criticks spread,
364 x Blackmore's Job.   And all was hush'd — v. 372.
         a waving sea of Heads.

Book the Second.

Or prouder march'd, with magistrates in state,
To some fam'd round-house, ever open gate!
How E——— lay inspir'd beside a sink,
380 And to mere mortals seem'd a Priest in drink?
All others timely, to the neighbouring *Fleet*
(Haunt of the Muses) made their safe retreat.

End of the Second Book.

[Manuscript annotations at top:]
First T——d sits in all his Glory crown'd,
With ev'ry Emblem of his Empire round
Fast by the Throne there Bridewell Lictors stand, Hore
The Bedlam Prophets in   Band.
                                          in dread order

[Right margin:]
In you thick Mist see Durfey not alone:
Each Modern Sense bows before his Throne.

[Left margin, vertical:]
Each Modern Tongue by its prophetique
Sleep them; Divining with short & Pike
Most happy Misery with Breeches long
much Cherub Holiday with sky & Pike
Releives by fits her long deathwatch

The Dunciad.

THE DUNCIAD.

Book the Third.

BUT in her *Temple*'s last recess inclos'd,
On *Dulness*' lap th' Anointed head repos'd.
Him close she curtain'd round with vapors
   blue,
And soft besprinkled with *Cimmerian* dew.
5 Then Raptures high the seat of sense o'erflow,
Which only heads refin'd from reason know:
Hence from the straw where *Bedlam*'s Prophet nods,
He hears loud Oracles, and talks with Gods;
Hence the Fool's paradise, the Statesman's scheme,
10 The air-built Castle, and the golden Dream,

The

[Left margin annotations:]
? T's honest holy spread,
was laid th' anointed Head
repos'd

well purg'd
on   as
high

[Below main text:]
v. 4, 5. And sprinkled o'er his Lids Lethean Dew;
O'er all his Brain extatic Raptures flow,
Hence for y* Straw Which only H. well-purg'd from Reason know air 1st
              He hears   Knowing the Holy Place,
A Thousand   watch'd
And glorious Visions of the mighty race.
In the soft arms of Sleep & Death convey'd,
He seems descended to th' Elysian Shade:
There in a dusky —— Old Bavius sits v. 15
xx Instant away they seiz'd, just shake their Ears
Knock at y* gate of Life (which Curl & Mears
post⌇ Set wide to all) assume a Calf-Skin dress,
Demanding Birth, impatient for the Press.
Million ——— v. 23.

these soon as dipt all instant take their flight
where Brown & Mears
Demanding there take new Bodies, & a Calfskin dress,

Book the Third.   37.

The Maids romantic wish, the Chymists flame,   *Maiden's reverie*
And Poets vision of eternal fame.

       swift
And now, on Fancy's easy wing convey'd,   *Hence swift*
The King descended to th' *Elyzian* shade.   *Monarch wanders in*
15 There in a dusky vale where *Lethe* rolls,
Old *Bavius* sits, to dip poetic souls,
And blunt the sense, and fit it for a skull
Of solid proof, impenetrably dull.
              take
Instant when dipt, away they wing their flight,
20 Where * *Brown* and *Mears* unbar the gates of Light,
Demand new bodies, and in Calf's array *Assume*   *:skin Dress,*
Rush to the world, impatient for the day.   *from ye Press.*
Millions and millions on these banks he views,
Thick as the Stars of night, or morning dews,   *as thick as Stars, as thick as*
25 As thick as bees o'er vernal blossoms fly,
As thick as eggs at W——d in pillory.   *round*
Wond'ring he gaz'd, when Bavius thus begun,
               grave
(" Wond'ring he gaz'd: When lo! a Sage appears,   *form*
By his broad shoulders known, and length of ears,

   * Booksellers.
       against   *Known*
2|v 17. *And proof to Sense, impenetrably dull, Proof to all*
 1| *With a chill an Thickness arms the Scull.*   *each*

v.27. *When lo! grave Settle's rev'rend form appears,*
    By his broad sh—
    known by his Band, & by the Suit he wore,

[Top marginal annotation:]
Amaz'd he stood, when Bavius thus begun,
With Speech familiar, as from Sire to Son.
O giv'n to see — v. 35.

38   The DUNCIAD.

[Left margin:] The Spreading Band,
Tessue
postpone

Known by the band and suit which *Settle* wore,
30 (His only suit) for twice three years before.
All as the Vest, appear'd the wearers frame,
Old in new state, another, yet the same.
Bland and familiar as in life, begun
Thus the great Father to the greater Son.

[Left margin:] giv'n

35 Oh! born to see what none can see awake!
Behold the wonders of th' *Oblivious Lake.*

[Left margin:] sacred

Thou, yet unborn, hast touch'd this sacred shore,
The hand of *Bavius* drench'd thee o'er and o'er.
But blind to former, as to future, *Fate,*

[Left margin:] Thou knowst not Son, thy
Thou knowst not how
down from Dutchm̃. into Dutc

40 What mortal knows his pre-existent state?
Who knows how long, thy transmigrating soul
Did from *Bœotian* to *Bœotian* roll? *Long frõ D.̃ down to D.̃*
      Thee sure
How many *Dutchmen* she vouchsaf'd to thrid?
How many stages thro' old *Monks* she rid?
45 And all who since, in mild benighted days,
Mix'd the Owl's ivy with the Poet's bays?
As Man's mæanders to the vital spring

[Left margin:] after v. 42.

Roll all their tydes, then back their circles bring;

[Handwritten text below, continuing in manuscript:]
Then turnd Ap-rice, Vandunck, & numbers more who Cambrian Leek or
For this. 53.   *Lawrel*
v. 38. these arms my [?]d *The sacred Bavius drench'd thee oer & oer*
I made thee proof to all the points of sense,
Impenetrable Dullness thy Defence
Know, unremembring of thy former state!
What Dullness grac'd thy pre-existent state:
Thou wert Ap-rice, Vandunck, & numbers more,
Who Cambrian Leek, or High dutch Lawrel wore.
                          Low
What tho no Bees around thy Cradle flew
Nor on thy lips distill'd their Golden Dew?
Yet have I left — — — in their stead,
   What swarms
A swarm of Drones have buzz'd about thy Head.
When thou, like Orpheus, strike [?] Lyre, warbli[ng]
How list'ning
Attentive Blocks stand round thee Bavius. Come then

[Right margin, vertical:] sworn Lawr[?] Aprice, Vandunck, & numb[ers] who Cambrian

Let scenes of glory past enflame thy mind,
How wide her Empire once, & unconfin'd.

Book the Third. 39

Or whirligigs, twirl'd round by skilful swain,
50 Suck the thread in, then yield it out again:
All nonsense thus, of old or modern date,
Shall in thee centre, from thee circulate.
For this, our ~~Queen~~ *Goddess* unfolds to vision true   *has purg'd*
Thy mental eye, (for thou hast much to view:)   *Scenes of old Glories,*
55 Old scenes of glory, times long cast behind,   *all her ancient reign*
Shall first recall'd, rush forward to thy mind;   *thus now   brain*
Then stretch thy sight o'er all her rising reign, *to triumphs yet behind.*
And let the past and future fire thy brain.   *Mind.*

Ascend this hill, whose cloudy point commands
60 Her boundless Empire ~~over~~ *spread o'er* seas and lands.   *stretch'd o'er*
See round the Poles where keener spangles shine,   *freezing Planets*
Where spices smoke beneath the burning Line,
(Earths wide extreams) her sable flag display'd;   *Sabled Ensign spread*
And all the nations cover'd in her shade!   *safe beneath*

add ⎰ 65 Far Eastward cast thy eye, from whence the *Sun*
     ⎱ And orient *Science* at a birth begun.
One man immortal all that pride confounds,   *Lo! He* ──
He, whose long *Wall* the wand'ring *Tartar* bounds. *That early dawn is*
             * Heav'ns! *Sudden Night surrounds*

Come then, (for Dulness sure across this grade)
Come & survey the Wonders of the Place.
Behold em all they saw, thus throws light   sight,
Survey thy Progeny, th' illustrious throng,
In Nature's Order as they move along.   rise to light.
Ascend this Mount, from whence thine Eye comands
Her Spacious Empire, spread o'er Seas & Lands,

40   The DUNCIAD.

*Heav'ns! what a pyle? whole ages perish there:
70 And one bright blaze turns Learning into air.

Thence to the South as far extend thy eyes;
There rival flames with equal glory rise,
From shelves to shelves † see greedy *Vulcan* roll,
And lick up all their *Physick* of the *Soul*.

75 How little, see! that portion of the ball,
Where, faint at best the beams of science fall!
Against her throne, from *Hyperborean* skies,
In dulness strong, th' avenging *Vandals* rise;
Lo where *Mæotis* sleeps, and hardly flows
80 The freezing *Tanais* thro' a waste of snows.
The North by myriads pours her mighty sons,
Great nurse of *Goths*, of *Alans*, and of *Huns*.
See *Alaric*'s stern port, the martial frame
Of *Genseric*, and *Attila*'s dread name!

---

* *Ho-am-ti*, Emperor of *China*, the same who built the great wall between *China* and *Tartary*, destroyed all the books, and learned men of that empire.

† The *Caliph*, *Omar* I. having conquer'd *Ægypt*, caus'd his General to burn the *Ptolomæan* library; on the gates of which was this inscription, *Medicina Animæ*.

Marginal annotations (left margin):
- thine
- swallow
- now
- short &
- streams of
- millions
- stern
- godlike

Marginal additions (bottom):
v. 77, 78.
Rebellious Europe parted from her Reign, See!
How soon she gather'd to her Wings again?
Southward as fast from Libya's torrid
Swift Lo! to her aid the Glorious Vandals fly.
As swift behold! from yet remoter skies,
In Dullness great the Glorious Vandals rise.

*Then from a Mountains Cloudy top the Guide
Shews all the Kingdoms of the Goddess wide
From whence the North first pour'd her mighty Sons,
Stern Nurse of Alans, Visigoths, & Huns:
Where dull Mæotis sleeps, & hardly flows,
The frozen Tanais thro' a waste of Snows.*

BOOK the THIRD. 41

85 See! the bold *Ostrogoths* on *Latium* fall;   *Millions of*
See! the fierce *Visigoths* on *Spain* and *Gaul*. *Millions of*
See! where the morning gilds the palmy shore,
(The soil that arts and infant letters bore)
His conq'ring tribes th' *Arabian* prophet draws,
90 And saving Ignorance enthrones by Laws.   *restores*
See *Christians*, *Jews*, one heavy sabbath keep;   *a*
And all the Western World believe and sleep.

Behold *Hostis iterum, once in Science proud Fatoe Basilea in one foggy cloud?*
Lo *Rome* herself, proud mistress now no more   *See the*
Of arts, but thund'ring against *Heathen* lore;
95 Her gray-hair'd Synods damning books unread,
And *Bacon* trembling for his brazen Head.
Lo statues, temples, theatres o'erturn'd,
(Oh glorious ruin!) and * * * burn'd.   *Varius / Vigilius*

See'st thou an *Isle*, by Palmers, Pilgrims trod,   *Beh'd. yon neighb'r. Isle, all over*
100 Men bearded, bald, cowl'd, uncowl'd, shod, unshod,   *In tracks of Pilgrim's. by feet*
Peel'd, patch'd, and pieball'd, linsey-woolsey brothers   *O'errun with*
Grave mummers, sleeveless some, and shirtless others.

*Who of both   & bath'd in Childrens Blood,
Yet fought for Easter, or a [stick] of wood That
Could weep devoutly when an Image spoke,
And groan in concert with a Saint of Oak.*

*Almighty Dullness! what a Sea of Blood
For early Easter, or a stick of wood
Thus visit not ——— Oh Spread — v. 108.*

*All this pursu'd the Sire, was once our own,
Now shorter Limits bound her Throne.*

42   The DUNCIAD.

That once was *Britain*— Happy! had she seen
No fiercer sons, had ‡ *Easter* never been.
105 In peace, great Goddess! ever be ador'd;
How keen the war, if dulness draw the sword?
Thus visit not thy own! on this blest age
Oh spread thy Influence, but restrain thy Rage!

And see my son, the hour is on its way
110 That lifts our Goddess to imperial sway:
This fav'rite Isle, long sever'd from her reign,
Dove-like, she gathers to her wings again.
Now look thro' Fate! behold the scene she draws!
What aids, what armies, to assert her cause!
115 See all her progeny, illustrious sight!
Behold, and count them as they rise to light.
As *Berecynthia*, while her offspring vye
In homage, to the mother of the sky,
Surveys around her in the blest abode
120 A hundred sons, and ev'ry son a God:

‡ Wars in *England* anciently, about the right time of celebrating *Easter*.

[Marginal MS notes:]
Nor   thus thine
The Hours   already wings
bear   parted
Their / our / the
Lo!
In natures order
pleas'd Cybele

v. 109. Here once more, son, but in a milder way,   Not
The Goddess meditates Imperial sway
The Time revolving, rip'ning takes Decree,
Much from her sons she hopes, & most from thee.
Then look thro' fate —   v 113.

Book the Third.   43

Not with less glory mighty *Dulness* crown'd, *triumph*
Shall take thro' *Grubstreet* her triumphant round,
And all *Parnassus* glancing o'er at once,
Behold a hundred sons, and each a dunce.

125 Mark first the youth who takes the foremost place
And thrusts his person full into your face,
With all thy Father's virtues blest, be born!
And a new C——*ibbe*r shall the stage adorn.

vanish'd to Modesty at Ed. 1736. p. 190. —— to   — *sighs return.*
                                                    Behold yon pair

See yet a younger, by his blushes known,
130 And modest as the maid who sips alone.
From the strong fate of drams if thou get free,
Another *Durfey*, *** shall sing in thee.
For thee each Ale-house, and each Gill-house mourn,
And answ'ring Gin-shops sowrer sighs return.

135 Behold yon pair, in strict embraces join'd;
How like their manners, and how like their mind!
Fam'd for good nature, B——*urnet* and for truth,
D——*ucket* for pious passion to the youth.

G 2   Equal

The DUNCIAD.

Equal in wit, and equally polite,
140 Shall this a *Pasquin*, that a *Grumbler* write;
Like are their merits, like rewards they share,
That shines a Consul, this Commissioner.

Ah D——[ennis], G——[ildon] ah! what ill-starr'd rage
Divides a friendship long confirm'd by age?
145 Blockheads with reason wicked wits abhor,
But fool with fool is barb'rous, civil war.
Embrace, embrace my Sons! be foes no more!
Nor glad vile Poets with true Criticks gore.

See next two slip-shod *Muses* traipse along,
150 In lofty madness meditating song,
With tresses staring from poetic dreams,
And never wash'd, but in *Castalia's* streams.
H—— and T——, glories of their race!
Lo H——ck's fierce, and M——'s rueful face!
155 W——n, the scourge of Scripture, mark with awe!
And mighty J——b Blunderbus of Law!
Lo thousand thousand, ev'ry nameless name,
All crowd, who foremost shall be damn'd to fame;

[marginalia:]
frantic
at the verge of
men of wit

again

With heads—
With Tresses
And never
H—d & W——y,
Concanen next, & Mitchell meet

aft. v. 154 One great of Stomach, Cook Horneck
And thousand thousand nameless names behind.

See Pix & Slip-shod W—— traipse along,
With heads unpinn'd, & meditating song &c—strea[ms]

Book the Third.

How proud! how pale! how earnest all appear! *Tedious all ye cheat*
160 How rhymes eternal gingle in their ear!

Pass these to nobler sights: Lo H---- stands *Behold amidst you crond*
Tuning his voice, and balancing his hands, *And tunes ....*
How honey'd nonsense trickles from his tongue!
How sweet the periods, neither said nor sung!
165 Still break the benches, H---- with thy strain, *only*
While K----t, Br----, W----n preach in vain
Round him, each *Science* by its modern type
Stands known; *Divinity* with box and pipe,
And proud *Philosophy* with breeches tore,
170 And *English Musick* with a dismal score:
While happier *Hist'ry* with her comrade *Ale*, *loud*
Sooths the sad series of her tedious tale.
Dull Woolston scourge of scripture mixt with awe,
And duller Jacob thunders of ye law.
Fast by, in darkness palpable inshrin'd
W----s, B----r, M----n, all the poring kind,
175 A lumberhouse of Books in every head,
Are ever reading, and are never read.

v. 165. *Pass these for nobler scenes, lo! yonder spread*
Lo! yonder must there a----
The fog where obscurest muse-full head.
But Mark where the thickest Darkness veils ye place,
Great great the poring
There Barnes, there Bentley, & their numerous race
a lumberhouse
With twice ten thousand volumes in their heads
Are never read.————v. 176.
pregnant clouds of thick'end
On yonder part what fogs of gather'd air
Invest the scene, there muse full sits Mahair.

[manuscript additions at top:]
> And lo! Start the Furies! sooty feinds advance,
> And lilly-handed Ladies joyn the dance.
> Now walk the Trees, now Rivers upward rise,
> Whales spout in Groves, & Dolphins in the skies.
> [Here, born off to v. 207. angel &c.]

† Corn field
on fire...

The DUNCIAD.

But who is he, in closet close y-pent,
With visage from his shelves with dust besprent?
Eye aredes — Right well mine eyes arede that myster wight,
180 That wonnes in haulkes and hernes, and *Wormius* he hight.
To future ages may thy dulness last,
As thou preserv'st the dulness of the past!

? / now Sir, to .... extend thine Eyes
wonders rise — But oh! what scenes, what miracles behind!
Extend thy Eyes, — Now stretch thy *Eye* view, and open all thy mind.

185 He look'd, and saw a sable * seer arise,
Swift to whose hand a winged volume flies.
All sudden, gorgons hiss, and dragons glare,
And ten horn'd fiends, and giants, threaten war.
Hell rises, heav'n descends, to dance on earth:
190 Gods, monsters, furies, musick; rage and mirth;
A fire, a jig, a battel, and a ball,
'Till one wide conflagration swallows all.

Thence
Then a new world to nature's laws unknown,
Refulgent rises, with a heav'n its own:

aft v. 184. Then wondrous — as Ed. 36 - 16. was Another
And Pegasean Horse come flying in
And justling Knights, in Panoply of Tin
Then from behind hat .... hop'd in ...... Then from
Appeard in a radiant cloud of Sarcenet white
For the beaming .... ing. For the beaming
Swift the rising Cynthia shed her Silver light
Then the brown shadows breaking ....
Then swiftly fleet the shades of Night away
And lo! Three suns illuminate the Day
those
three tapers raise at pleasure highest,
Illuminate their light, & set their flames on fire
Earthquakes — Thick Darkness blots out those: then downward pours
M. Aetna — Wide ore the darkned Landscape, snow or showrs.
Upstart. Supra Earthquakes. M. Aetna.

Book the Third. 47

195 Another *Cynthia* her new journey runs,
   And other planets circle other suns:
   The forests dance, the rivers upward rise,
   Whales sport in woods, and dolphins in the skies;
   And last, to give the whole creation grace,
200 Lo! one vast *Egg* produces human race.

   Silent the monarch gaz'd; yet ask'd in thought
   What God or Dæmon all these wonders wrought?
   To whom the Sire: In yonder cloud, behold,
   Whose sarcenet skirts are edg'd with flamy gold,
205 A godlike youth: See *Jove*'s own bolts he flings,
   Rolls the loud thunder, and the light'ning wings!
   Angel of *Dulness*, sent to scatter round
   Her magic charms on all unclassic ground:
   Yon stars, yon suns, he rears at pleasure higher,
210 Illumes their light, and sets their flames on fire.
   Immortal R—ch! how calm he sits at ease,
   Mid snows of paper, and fierce hail of peafe?
   And proud his mistress' orders to perform,
   Rides in the whirlwind, and directs the storm.

The DUNCIAD.

215 But lo! to dark encounter in mid'air,
New wizards rise: here B——th, and C——r there.
B——th in his cloudy tabernacle shrin'd,
On grinning dragons C——r mounts the wind:
Dire is the conflict, dismal is the din,
220 Here shouts all *Drury*, there all *Lincoln's-Inn*;
Contending Theatres our empire raise,
Alike their labours, and alike their praise.

And are these wonders, Son, to thee unknown?
Unknown to thee? These wonders are thy own.
225 These Fate reserv'd to grace thy reign divine,
Foreseen by me, but ah! with-held from mine.
In *Lud*'s old walls tho' long I rul'd renown'd,
Far as loud *Bow*'s stupendous bells resound;
Tho' my own Aldermen conferr'd my bays,
230 To me committing their eternal praise,
Their full-fed Heroes, their pacific May'rs,
Their annual trophies, and their monthly wars:

Marginalia (left margin): her / shouts there bellows / Her / ——

Marginalia (bottom):
v. 215. See opposite, with Cibber at his side,
Booth in his cloudy Tabernacle sides. Tho'
On flying Dragons, & in the Clouds of air,
Seer wars with Seer, here Rich, & Cibber there.
with flying Dragons Cibber; see beside by his side,
[No more Ms]

BOOK the THIRD.   49

Tho' † long my Party built on me their hopes,
For writing Pamphlets, and for roasting *Popes*.
235 (Different our parties, but with equal grace
Our Goddess smiles on *Whig* and *Tory* race,
'Tis the same rope at sev'ral ends they twist,
To *Dulness, Ridpath* is as dear as *Mist*.)
Yet lo! in me what Authors have to brag on!
240 Reduc'd at last to hiss in my own dragon.
Avert it, heav'n! that thou or C———r e'er
Should wag two serpent tails in *Smithfield* fair.
Like the vile straw that's blown about the streets,
The needy Poet sticks to all he meets,
245 Coach'd, carted, trod upon, now loose, now fast,
In the Dog's tail his progress ends at last.
Happier thy fortunes! like a rolling stone
Thy giddy dulness still shall lumber on,
Safe in its heaviness, can never stray,
250 And licks up every blockhead in the way.

† *Settle* was once famous for party papers, but very uncertain in his political principles. He was employ'd to hold the pen in the *Character of a popish successor*, but afterwards printed his *Narrative* on the contrary side.
He managed the ceremony and pageants at the burning of a famous *Pope*, and was at length employ'd in making the machinery at *Bartholomew* fair, where, in his old age he acted in a dragon of leather of his own invention.

H   Thy

Thy dragons * * and * * shall taste,
And from each show rise duller than the last:
'Till rais'd from Booths to Theatre, to Court,
Her seat imperial Dulness shall transport.
255 (Already, *Opera* prepares the way,
The sure fore-runner of her gentle sway.)
To aid her cause, if heav'n thou canst not bend,
Hell thou shalt move; for *Faustus* is thy friend:
Pluto with *Cato* thou for her shalt join,
260 And link the *Mourning-Bride* to *Proserpine*.
Grubstreet! thy fall should men and Gods conspire,
Thy stage shall stand, ensure it but from Fire.
Another *Æschylus* appears! prepare
For new * Abortions, all ye pregnant fair!
265 In flames like *Semele* be brought to bed,
While opening Hell spouts wild-fire at your head.

Now *Bavius* take the poppy from thy brow,
And place it here! here all ye Heroes bow!

* It is reported of *Æschylus* that when his Tragedy of the *Eumenides* was acted, the audience were so terrified that the children fell into fits, and the bigbelly'd women miscarry'd. T———d is translating this Author.

This.

Book the Third.

This, this is He, foretold by ancient rhymes,
270 Th' *Augustus*, born to bring *Saturnian* times!
Beneath his reign, shall E———n wear the bays, *Eusden*
C———r preside, Lord Chancellor of Plays, *Cibber*
B——— sole judge of Architecture sit, *Benson*
And A——e P——s be preferr'd for Wit! *Amb. Philips*
275 I see th' unfinish'd *Dormitory* wall!
I see the *Savoy* totter to her fall!
The sons of *Isis* reel! the towns-mens sport,
And *Alma Mater* all dissolv'd in *Port*!

Then, when these signs declare the mighty Year,
280 When the dull Stars roll round, and re-appear;
Let there be darkness! (the dread pow'r shall say)
All shall be darkness, as it ne'er were Day;
To their first Chaos Wit's vain works shall fall,
And universal Dulness cover all!

285 No more the Monarch could such raptures bear;
He wak'd, and all the Vision mix'd with air.

FINIS.

Book the Third. 85

This, this is He, foretold by ancient rhymes,
270 Th' Augustus, born to bring Saturnian times!
 Beneath his reign, shall E——n when the boys
 C——r preside, Lord Chancellor of Plays,
 B—— (ole judge of Architecture fit,
 And A—— P— be preferr'd for Wit!
275 I see th' unfinish'd Dormitory wall!
 I see the Savoy totter to her fall!
 The sons of Is: reel! the towns-mens foot,
 And Alma Mater all diffolv'd in Port!

 Then, when these signs declare the mighty Year,
280 When the dull Stars roll round, and re-appear:
 Let there be darkness! (the dread pow'r shall say)
 All shall be darkness, as it ne'er were Day;
 To their first Chaos Wit's vain works shall fall,
 And universal Dulness cover all!

285 No more the Monarch could such raptures bear;
 He wak'd, and all the VISION was with air.

FINIS.

Appendixes
Index

APPENDIX 1

Collation of the Authorized 1728 Impressions

The following lists register variations in the *Dunciad*s produced by James Bettenham in 1728. According to title-page designations, the group includes the duodecimo and octavo issues of what was implicitly the "first edition" (*Foxon* P764–65; "1a" and "1b" here); the "Second Edition" (P766; "2"); the first "Third Edition," with a flower vase ornament (P767; "3a"); and a second "Third Edition," with the ornament of Justice (P768; "3b"). The records are based on my examination of sixty-seven copies of these impressions, thirty-four of which I have compared on the Hinman Collator or Lindstrand Comparator. I have found no variant formes in the octavo and only a few of them (specified in the lists) within other printings.

Text

The first table records alterations in the text itself. (The form represented by the Berg copy appears in column 1b.) Any material that occurs for the first time is written out; any repeated from the preceding printing is represented by a dash. To highlight the point of variation when only punctuation changes, a swung dash (~) signifies the repetition of a word from the previous reading and a caret (˄) marks the absence of a punctuation mark. The long ess is not distinguished, and brackets enclose editorial matter. Page and line numbers refer to the Berg copy presented in facsimile. When later printings add footnotes the readings may appear on an adjacent page, but the line references make them easy to find.

Appendix 1

The table makes it possible to tell at a glance the nature of the alterations, the point at which variations occurred, and the relative frequency of such modifications in any of the printings. It furnishes the evidence (now expanded) which over the years has been the chief grounds for debate about the printing order. It also provides opportunity to consider the interesting bibliographical question of whether texts improve or deteriorate as they are reproduced. It does not record adjustments in the title-page edition statements, variations in printer's ornaments, changes in the symbols that signal footnotes, alterations between stars and asterisks or between dashes and groups of hyphens, or differences in the length of dashes (which varies arbitrarily). The number of hyphens used on the seven occasions in the octavo printing where they substitute for letters in names seems without significance, though on the chance that they might point to the number of missing characters they are worth noting: 1.116 *W* [2 hyphens] *y*; 2.368 *S* [5 hyphens]; 3.155 *W* [5 hyphens] *n*; 3.161 *H* [4 hyphens]; 3.165 *H* [4 hyphens]; 3.166 *W* [7 hyphens]; 3.216 *C* [4 hyphens] *r*.

The new impressions were largely from standing type, entailing that their alterations tended to result from a volitional act by the author or printer (though the text would also be subject to inadvertent changes during handling). On the other hand, some sections were reset: in the "Second Edition," gathering B, most of C (1–3, some of 4ᵛ, most of 6ʳ), and D4ᵛ; in 3a, gathering E; and in 3b, gathering B. In these places there is a greater chance that the changes were unintentional.

The Twickenham Edition records nearly all of the fifty or so differences in wording, though it cites virtually none of the changes in punctuation, capitalization, spelling, or use of roman and italic—for which Pope may also have been responsible. In a couple of instances that edition misidentifies the point at which new readings enter, and twice (A.2.331 and 341) it identifies "1728" readings found in no copies I have examined.

Appendix 1

Sig. 12° 8°	Page/Line	1a (12°)	1b (8°)	2 (12°)	3a (12°)	3b (12°)
A2ʳ a2ʳ	Title	DUBLIN	—	DUDLIN / DUBLIN [varies]	DUBLIN	—
A3ʳ a3ʳ	iii.10	to be but	—	—	but to be	—
A4ʳ a4ʳ	v.15	affected,	—	~)	—	—

Book 1

Sig. 12° 8°	Page/Line	1a (12°)	1b (8°)	2 (12°)	3a (12°)	3b (12°)
B1ʳ B1ʳ	1.pag	1	—	[absent in some copies]	1	—
	1.1	BOOKS	BOOK	BOOKS	—	—
B1ᵛ B1ᵛ	2.15	[indented]	—	—	—	[flush]
	2.24	*Quidnunc's*	*Quidnunc's*	—	—	—
	2.28	*L——t's*	—	—	*L——'s*	—
B2ʳ B2ʳ	3.35	*Fortitude*	—	Fortitude	—	*Fortitude*
	3.39	jayl;	—	—	—	~ :
	3.45	45	—	—	54	45
B2ᵛ B2ᵛ	4.59	him self	himself	—	—	—
	4.64	Fast by, fair	—	There painted	—	—
	4.66	harvests	—	harvest	—	harvests
B3ʳ B3ʳ	5.71	monsters	—	—	—	Monsters
	5.72	fools-colours	—	—	—	~ ˄ ~
	5.73n1	*Geo. Tho*——	—	*George Tho*—— *Lord Mayor of London.*	—	—
	5.74n1	general	—	—	—	General
	5.74n2	victory	—	—	—	Victory
	5.76	broadfaces	broad faces	—	—	—
	5.78	Yet	—	—	—	But
	5.79	in pleasing slumbers	—	—	—	all hush'd and satiate
	5.80	And	—	—	—	Yet

Appendix 1

Sig. 12° 8°	Page/Line	1a (12°)	1b (8°)	2 (12°)	3a (12°)	3b (12°)
	5.81	But	—	—	—	While
	5.84	city-*Swans*	—	City-*Swans*	—	—
	5.85	antient	—	—	—	ancient
	5.85n4	Enterludes	Interludes	Enterludes	—	—
B3ᵛ B3ᵛ	6.90	lump,	—	—	—	~ ˰
	6.91	in *N——n* all his father	—	old *Pryn* in restless *Daniel*	—	—
	6.94	*D——n*	—	*D——s*	—	—
	6.94	*Wh——*'s	—	*W——*'s	—	*W——y*'s
	6.95	95	—	—	—	25
	6.96	in *Tibbald*'s	in *Tibbald*'s	—	—	—
	6.98	hell,	—	~ ˰	—	—
	6.98	battels	—	battles	battels	battle's
	6.98n2	See	—	See	—	—
	6.98n2	170	—	185	—	—
	6.101	books	—	—	—	Books
	6.103	there:	—	~ ,	—	—
	6.104	writ,	—	—	—	~ ˰
	6.104	on,	—	—	—	~ ˰
B4ʳ B4ʳ	7.111	*great*,	—	—	—	~ :
	7.116	*W——y*, *W——s*, and *Bl——*˰	—	*W——s*, *Q——s*, and *Bl——*˰	—	*Withers, Quarles,* and *Blome.*
	7.118	age	—	Age	—	—
	7.119	˰ *Caxton*	—	* ~	—	—
	7.119n	[no note]	—	*Old Printers.	—	—
	7.120	cow-hide:	—	—	—	~ :
	7.122	philosophy	Philosophy	philosophy	—	—
	7.124	˰ *Philemon*	—	§*Philemon*	—	—
	7.124n	[no note]	—	§*Philemon Holland.*	—	—
B4ᵛ B4ᵛ	8.125	125	—	—	—	127
	8.125	size	—	—	—	Size
	8.130	base:	—	—	—	~ ;
	8.131	lessening	—	lessoning	—	—

Appendix 1

Sig. 12° 8°	Page/Line	1a (12°)	1b (8°)	2 (12°)	3a (12°)	3b (12°)
	8.137	Oh	—	—	—	O
	8.137	thou!	—	—	—	~ ˰
	8.142	mind,	—	~ .	—	—
	8.cw	Ah!	~ ˰	~ !	—	—
B5ʳ C1ʳ	9.146	land,	—	~ .	—	—
	9.148	show	—	—	—	shew
	9.149	*scholiasts*	—	Scholiasts	—	—
	9.151	Moderns	—	—	—	Modern
	9.158	Prologues	—	prologues	—	—
	9.159	'till	—	˰ till	—	—
	9.163	pen	—	quill	—	—
	9.163	criticks	—	Critiques	—	—
	9.164	verse	—	Verse	—	—
	9.165	written	—	graver	—	gravest
	9.cw	As	A	A / As [varies]	As	—
B5ᵛ C1ᵛ	10.167	it self	itself	it self	—	itself
	10.168	thro'	thro '	thro'	—	—
	10.172	Elasticity,	—	~ ˰	—	—
	10.174	state.	—	—	—	~ ,
	10.179	*Flaccus*˰	—	—	~ .	~ ˰
	10.180	*guide*	—	Guide	—	—
B6ʳ C2ʳ	11.190	W——	—	—	—	W——d
B6ʳ C2ᵛ	12.204	*Thulè*	—	Thule	—	—
	12.204	Bed	—	—	—	bed
	12.205	pyre;	—	~ :	—	~:
	12.210	herself	—	—	—	her self
	12.212	home:	—	~ .	—	—
	12.214	place:	—	—	—	~ :
	12.217	Chosen	—	chosen	—	—
C1ʳ C3ʳ	13.222	those	—	—	—	these
	13.222	away:	—	~ ·. [colon slants left]	—	—
	13.235	again ˰	—	—	~ ,	—
	13.240	H——	—	—	—	H——d
C1ᵛ C3ᵛ	14.241	sons ˰	—	—	—	~:

Appendix 1

Sig. 12° 8°	Page/Line	1a (12°)	1b (8°)	2 (12°)	3a (12°)	3b (12°)
	14.242	puns:	—	—	—	~ ˄
	14.244	˄Till	—	' ~	—	—
	14.end	*first*	—	First	—	—

Book 2

Sig. 12° 8°	Page/Line	1a (12°)	1b (8°)	2 (12°)	3a (12°)	3b (12°)
C2ᵛ C4ᵛ	16.10	prizes	—	—	—	Prizes
	16.15	authors	—	—	—	Authors
	16.15	stationers	—	—	—	Stationers
C3ʳ D1ʳ	17.29	[flush]	—	—	—	[indented]
	17.29	strain;	—	~ !	—	—
	17.33	said˄	—	—	—	~ ,
	17.42	C——l.	—	~ ,	—	—
C3ᵛ D1ᵛ	18.57	slide:	—	~ ;	—	—
	18.59	varlet	—	—	—	Miscreant
	18.60	lay'd:	—	~ ;	—	—
C4ʳ D2ʳ	19.79	vot'ry's	—	Vot'ry's	—	—
C4ᵛ D2ᵛ	20.89	victor	—	—	—	Victor
	20.106	**, **, and **,	—	—	—	B—— ˄ B—— ˄ B—— ,
	20.106	wretches	—	—	—	Varlets
	20.cw	C——l,	~ ˄	~ ,	—	~ ˄
C5ʳ D3ʳ	21.124	**'s	—	—	—	D——on's
C5ᵛ D3ᵛ	22.127	˄pillory'd	—	* ~	—	—
	22.127n	[no note]	—	[Curl note]	—	—
	22.143	fair-streaming	—	—	—	far- ~
	22.	[ll. 125–43]	—	[ll. 125–41]	—	—
	22.cw	"His	—	The	—	—
C6ʳ D4ʳ	23.	[ll. 144–63]	—	[ll. 142–63]	—	—
	23.153	labor'd	—	labour'd	—	—
	23.159	Spirits	—	Spirts	—	—

Appendix 1

Sig. 12° 8°	Page/Line	1a (12°)	1b (8°)	2 (12°)	3a (12°)	3b (12°)
D1r E1r	25.186	**	—	—	—	T——
	25.195	in Pray'r	—	and ~	—	—
D1v E1v	26.218	And R——, and railing	—	Noise, Noncence, N——n,	~ , Nonsense, ~ ,	—
	26.219	art	—	Art	—	—
	26.220	snip-snap	—	Snip-snap	—	—
	26.220	interruption	—	Interruption	—	—
D2r E2r	27.229	So	—	Sore	—	—
D2v E2v	28.242	.H——d	—	—	—	†*Hunger-ford*
	28.242n	[no note]	—	—	—	†*Hunger-ford-Stairs.*
	28.260	hands:	—	~ ˄	—	—
D3r E3r	29.263	height,	—	~ ˄	—	—
	29.277	*** and ***	—	—	—	R—— and Wh——y
	29.cw	Thi	This	—	—	—
D3v E3v	30.280	Nor	—	Not	—	—
	30.281	W——d	—	—	—	We——d
	30.292	declares,	—	~ .	—	—
	30.294	in,	—	—	~:	—
D4r E4r	31.300	300	—	00	300	—
	31.310	Sh——	—	—	—	*Shadwell*
	31.311	M——n	—	*Milbourn*	—	—
D4v E4v	32.317	mov'd	—	moves	—	—
	32.325	325	—	525	325	—
	32.327	pow'r	—	Power	—	—
D5r F1r	33.353	T——d	—	—	—	*Toland*
D5v F1v	34.365	C——re	—	—	—	*Centlivre*
	34.372–73	[leaded]	—	—	[not leaded]	[leaded]
	34.373	[flush]	—	—	—	[indented]

149

Appendix 1

Book 3

E1ʳ F3ʳ	37.12	fame.	—	—	~ ,	—
	37.19	flight	—	—	fight	flight
	37.23	and millions	—	—	~ Millions	—
	37.28	broad ˏ shoulders	—	—	broad-shoulders	—
E1ᵛ F3ᵛ	38.31	wearers	—	wearer's	—	—
	38.39	future,	—	—	—	~ ˏ
	38.39	*Fate*	—	—	—	Fate
	38.48	tydes	—	—	tides	—
E2ʳ F4ʳ	39.61	where	—	—	were	—
	39.63	Earths	—	Earth's	—	—
E2ᵛ F4ᵛ	40.69	there:	—	—	~ ;	—
	40.75	see	—	—	—	mark
E3ʳ G1ʳ	41.	[ll. 85–102]	—	—	[ll. 85–104]	—
	41.98	***	—	—	—	*Apelles*
	41.101	brothers ˏ	—	—	—	~ ,
	41.104n	[Easter note on p. 42]	—	—	[Easter note on p. 41]	—
	41.cw	That	—	—	In	—
E3ᵛ G1ᵛ	41.	[ll. 103–20]	—	—	[ll. 105–24]	—
	42.106	war,	—	—	~ ˏ	~ ,
	42.106	draw	—	—	whet	—
	42.108	Oh	—	—	O	—
	42.109	son	—	—	Son	—
	42.104n	[Easter note on p. 42]	—	—	[Easter note on p. 41]	—
	42.cw	Not	—	—	Mark	—
E4ʳ G2ʳ	43.	[ll. 121–38]	—	—	[ll. 125–42]	—
	43.121	crown'd,	—	—	—	~ ˏ
	43.138	pious passion	—	—	—	cordial friendship
	43.cw	Equal	—	—	Ah	—

Appendix 1

Sig. 12° 8°	Page/Line	1a (12°)	1b (8°)	2 (12°)	3a (12°)	3b (12°)
E4ᵛ G2ᵛ	44.	[ll. 139–58]	—	—	[ll. 143–60]	—
	44.154	M——'s	—	—	—	R——me's
	44.154	rueful	—	—	—	peculiar
	44.155	Scripture	—	—	—	Gospel
	44.156	J——b.	—	—	~ ,	—
	44.cw	How	—	—	Pass	—
	44.160	rhymes	—	—	Rhymes	—
E5ʳ G3ʳ	45.	[ll. 159–76]	—	—	[ll. 161–78]	—
	45.161	H——	—	—	—	He——y
	45.165	H—— .	—	—	—	He——y,
	45.166	vain .	—	—	~ .	—
	45.170	score:	—	—	~ ;	—
	45.173	inshrin'd.	—	—	~ ,	—
	45.174	M——n	—	—	M——	—
E5ᵛ G3ᵛ	46.	[ll. 177–94]	—	—	[ll. 179–94]	—
	46.185n	[no note]	—	—	[Faustus note]	—
	46.185n3	[no note]	—	—	1728, all	~ . All
E6ᵛ G4ᵛ	48.218	wind:	—	—	~ ;	—
	48.232	wars:	—	—	~ :	—
F1ʳ H1ʳ	49.233n7	age .	—	—	~ ,	—
	49.233n7–8	dragon of leather	—	leathern dragon	—	—
F1ᵛ H1ᵛ	50.251	dragons . ** and **	—	—	—	~ , Magistrates and Peers
	50.263	prepare	—	Prepare	—	—
F2ʳ H2ʳ	51.273	B——	—	B——n	—	—
	51.277	towns-mens [long 's' / short 's']	towns-mens [short 's' / short 's']	—	—	—
F2ᵛ H2ᵛ	52.	[advert.]	[no advert.]	—	—	—

Appendix 1

Footnotes

By design the Twickenham Edition collates only selected versions of Pope's footnotes; among the omissions are the forms that appeared in 1728. The notes in the first two issues, and later variations within these, are available from the facsimile and from the collation table above. The five notes added in later impressions seem not to have been reprinted since 1728. Three of these are quoted in the table, at 7.119, 7.124, and 28.242. Two longer annotations here follow: the first appeared in the "Second Edition" and the other in printing 3a, though the asterisk used in the text to signal its presence had also occurred in all earlier impressions. Once inserted, both of these notes remained in the subsequent impressions (though the latter has a variant, listed in the collation table).

22.127: *It appears from hence that Mr. *Curl* had not himself stood in the *Pillory* when this Poem was writ, which happen'd not till *March*, 1728. at *Charing-Cross*.

46.185:*Dr. *Faustus* the subject of a sett of Farces, which with *Pluto* and *Proserpine*, &c. lasted in vogue two or three seasons at both Playhouses, in the years 1726, 1727, and 1728, all the extravagancies in the sixteen lines following, were actually introduced on the Stage, and frequented by the first Quality of *England*, to the twentieth and thirtieth times, 'till they were all swallow'd up in the *Beggar's Opera*.

Ornaments

Though not part of the verbal text, the type ornaments were imposed and printed along with the words and further illustrate the relationships among the 1728 impressions. The code here for each ornament consists of two elements: a mnemonic initial to indicate its kind (H[eadpiece], T[ailpiece], F[actotum]), and a number to identify its variety and, roughly, its order of appearance. An asterisk marks the first appearance of a particular ornament in this series of *Dunciad*s.

Appendix 1

12º	8º	Page	1a, 1b	2	3a	3b
A2ʳ	a2ʳ	Title	*T1	*T4	*T6	T7
A3ʳ	a3ʳ	iii	*F1	F1	F1	*F6
B1ʳ	B1ʳ	1	*H1	H2	H2	H3
B1ʳ	B1ʳ	1	*F2	F2	F2	*F7
C1ᵛ	C3ᵛ	14	*T2	T2	T6	*T8
C2ʳ	C4ʳ	15	*H2	H3	H3	H2
C2ʳ	C4ʳ	15	*F3	*F5	F5	F8
D6ʳ	F2ʳ	35	*T3	*T5	*T7	*T9
D6ᵛ	F2ᵛ	36	*H3	H2	H2	*H4
D6ᵛ	F2ᵛ	36	*F4	F4	F4	F3

Signatures

In addition to the alterations in the text itself, the pattern of signatures has figured in the debate over the priority of issues. The signing varies according to whether the book was imposed for duodecimo or octavo, and it is conventional—except that B3 in the octavo is also marked, probably because the printer did not bother to remove the type after the forme had been printed in duodecimo. The books are signed as follows:

12º: $1–3 (−A1, 2, F2)
8º: $1–2 (−a, b2, H2; +B3)

The relationship between signatures in the two formats can be determined from the left-hand columns in the collation table.

Press Figures

The pattern of press figures differs for each impression. This record of each pressman's role in printing the formes provides further help in analyzing the production of the book.

Appendix 1

12° 8°	Page	1a (12°)	1b (8°)	2 (12°)	3a (12°)	3b (12°)
A3ᵛ *a3ᵛ*	iv	1	1	1	3	2
B1ᵛ	2			3	2	4
4ʳ B4ʳ	7	1	4			
C4ᵛ	16		3			
C6ᵛ D4ᵛ	24	3	2	4	3	
D1ᵛ E1ᵛ	26		2	2	4	4
6ᵛ	36	4				
E1ᵛ F3ᵛ	38	2	2	3		
G4ʳ	47		1			
6ᵛ	48					4
F1ᵛ	50	3 [some copies]				

Paper

The Berg copy of the 1728 octavo is printed on the same varieties of paper that occur throughout the other exemplars of that issue. In those copies I have identified eight kinds of half sheets, plus a few strays. All have so-called double chain lines (the widely spaced lines in the leaf look like sets of miniature railroad tracks), with one of the chains consistently more pronounced than the other; the double chains indicate the paper probably was made in Genoa. Four of the half sheets have the watermark "BF" (present in gatherings b, B, F, G, and H in the Berg copy), and four are unmarked. The varieties can be further distinguished according to the relationship of the bold and vaguer chain lines. In two instances the dominant one is to the left with respect to the watermark letters when read correctly, and in the other two it is to the right. Similarly for the unmarked half sheets: two of them have the major chain nearer the outside, deckled edge, and two of them have it to the inner, or cut, edge.

The parallels between the eight marked and unmarked half sheets suggest that they are the sections of a set of four full sheets. That is confirmed by evidence from the duodecimo

Appendix 1

copies, which were printed on the same paper. (The paper of editions 2, 3a, and 3b is different.) Because of the imposition pattern of duodecimos, up to two-thirds (instead of only one-half) of the sheet is available in a gathering. When the variable distances between chain lines are measured and charted, the inner portions of pairs of marked and unmarked sections of these "two-thirds sheets" can be seen to overlap (in ways that are consistent with the pattern of dominant chain lines)—yielding four full sheets of paper. This number and the presence of tranchefiles (i.e., narrowly spaced chain lines) at only one end of each sheet match the characteristics which Philip Gaskell says distinguish paper produced by end-to-end two-sheet moulds (*A New Introduction to Bibliography* [1972; reprint with corrections, Oxford: Clarendon, 1974], 64). If such moulds were used for this paper, they antedate the earliest known ones in England by forty years and in France by sixty (Gaskell, 64).

APPENDIX 2

The Texts of the Unauthorized Editions of 1728

Two unauthorized editions of *The Dunciad* appeared within months of the original publication: the so-called "Gold chains" edition (*Foxon* P769), possibly published in Edinburgh, and one produced in Ireland by a group of Dublin booksellers (P770). Each used the first London duodecimo for its setting copy. Both have features of special interest to students of *The Dunciad*, but they also merit attention for what they reveal about the practices of printers when confronted with texts that they might be expected to reproduce literally.

The "Gold chains" edition derives its name from the reading in 1.76, an error for "glad chains" that Pope pointed out in a note to 1.86 of the *Dunciad Variorum*. It generally follows the text of the first duodecimo except that it has "Interludes" rather than "Enterludes" in the footnote on page 5. If the difference is not coincidental, it may have resulted, as Griffith suggests, from a copy of the octavo becoming available after the text had been set from the duodecimo. Such a situation occurred in the case of the first edition of Curll's *Key*, for instance, which was based on Bettenham's "first edition" but which on the last page added a reading from the newly available "second edition." The text of the "Gold chains" version differs from Bettenham's first duodecimo primarily in two respects: it consistently prints the first word of each verse paragraph (as well as "God" at 1.226) in regular and small capitals,

Appendix 2

and it capitalizes most of the common nouns—nearly 1,400—that Bettenham had put in lower case.

The chief interest of the Dublin reprint lies in the names it selects to fill Pope's blanks. Often they are consistent with ones Pope intended, at least when his design can be ascertained, but they sometimes differ dramatically. As a guide to Pope's possible targets, but more importantly as an indication of how the poem was read by a contemporary audience at some distance from London, I provide a collation of Pope's asterisks and initials with their Dublin renditions (without distinguishing the long ess), keyed to the Berg facsimile. The Dublin editors fail to fill the blanks at 2.106, 124, 186, 275, 277, 366, 367, 368, and 3.98, 132, 161, 165, 166, 174 (B——r and M——n), 180, 251.

Publisher to Reader

vi.22	Geo. Tho——ld] *George Thorald*
vii.23	W——] *Welsted*
vii.23	D——] *Dennis*
vii.23	R—— B——] *Richard Blackmore*

Book 1

2.28	C——l's] *Curl's*
2.28	L——t's] *Lintot's*
5.73	Tho——d] *Thorold*
5.73n1	Tho——] *Thorold*
6.91	N——n] *Nelson*
6.92	E——n] *Eusden*
6.92	Bl——'s] *Blackmore's*
6.93	P——s] *Philips*
6.93	T——te's] *Tate's*
6.94	D——n] *Dryden*

Appendix 2

Book 1

6.94	Wh——'s] *Wharton's*
7.116	W——y] *Westley*
7.116	W——s] *Wats*
7.116	Bl——] *Bloom*
11.190	W——] *Ward*
11.198n	T——d] *Theobald*
13.230	C——r] *Cibber*
13.230	Jo——n] *Johnson*
13.230	O——ll] *Ozell*
13.234	H——] *Hungerford*
13.240	G——n] *Gildon*
13.240	B——] *Bloom*
13.240	H——] *Howard*

Book 2

17.34	M——] *Moor*
17.37	L——t] *Lintot*
17.40	L——t] *Lintot*
17.42	C——l] *Curl*
17.46	L——t] *Lintot*
18.51	L——t] *Lintot*
18.54	C——l's] *Curl's*
18.57	C——l] *Curl*
18.58	L——t, L——t] *Lintot, Lintot*
18.66n	C——l's] *Curl's*
18.66n	L——t's] *Lintot's*
20.87	L——t] *Lintot*
20.94	C——l] *Curl*
20.96	G——] *Gay*
20.96	Y——] *Young*
20.96	S——] *Swift*

Appendix 2

Book 2

21.107	C——l]	Curl
21.118	C——]	Clarke
21.118	C——n]	Concanon
21.108n1	C——l]	Curl
22.127	D——]	Defoe
22.128	T——]	Tibbald
22.129	R——]	Rolli
23.148	Ch——d]	Ch——ud
23.148	C——l]	Curl
23.152	C——d]	Ch——ud
23.160	C——l]	Curl
24.170	Ch——d]	Ch——ud
25.184	R——]	Rolli
25.188	O——]	Oldisworth
25.190	O——]	Oldisworth
26.218	R——]	Rich
26.218	B——]	Brevall
26.219	D——s]	Dennis
27.229	G——t]	Gilbert
27.235	Bl——'s]	Blackmore's
28.242	H——d]	Hungerford
28.256	***]	Craftsman's
28.259	D——]	Dennis
29.267	E——]	Eusden
29.269	E——]	Eusden
29.270	E——]	Eusden
29.271	H——]	Hughes
30.280	Bl——]	Blackmore
30.281	W——d]	Welsted
30.288	E——]	Eusden
31.310	Sh——]	Shadwell
31.311	M——n]	Methwin
32.324	H——'s]	Haywood's
32.324	Bl——'s]	Blackmore's

159

Appendix 2

Book 2

33.351	B——l]	Blackmore
33.353	C——s]	Collins
33.353	T——d]	Toland
34.365	C——re]	Centlivre
34.368	S——]	Savage
34.369	N——n]	Nelson
35.379	E——]	Eusden

Book 3

37.26	W——d]	Ward
43.128	C——r]	Cibber
43.137	B——]	Burnet
43.138	D——]	Ducket
44.143	D——]	Dennis
44.143	G——]	Gildon
44.153	H——]	Howard
44.153	T——]	Tibbald
44.154	H——ck's]	Horneck's
44.154	M——'s]	Maxwell's
44.155	W——n]	Whiston
44.156	J——b]	Jacob
45.174	W——s]	Wats
47.211	R——ch]	Rich
48.216	B——th]	Booth
48.216	C——r]	Cibber
48.217	B——th]	Booth
48.218	C——r]	Cibber
49.241	C——r]	Cibber
50.264n3	T——d]	Tibbald
51.271	E——n]	Ecyden
51.272	C——r]	Cibber
51.273	B——]	Blondel
51.274	A——e P——s]	Ambrose Philips

APPENDIX 3

Varieties and States of the Altar Frontispiece

The plate used for the frontispiece of Bettenham's 1728 printings of *The Dunciad* was modified and reused in successive editions through 1736. In addition, the illustration was pirated in the "Gold chains" edition. The table overleaf records the metamorphosis of the design. As in the collation list, readings are represented by dashes when they repeat the previous form.

Appendix 3

Varieties and States of

	1.i	1.ii
Banner	THE | DUNCI-|AD	THE | DUNCIAD | VARIORUM
Book 6	P. & K. Arthur	—
Book 5	Shakeſp. Reſtor'd	—
Book 4	OGIL|BY	—
Book 3	Dennis's Works	—
Book 2	NEW|CAS|TLE	—
Book 1	Cibber's Plays	—
Imprint	DUBLIN; Printed; LONDON; Reprinted *for* A. Dodd	[deleted]
Occurrences (with *Foxon* number):	1728 12° and 8° (P764–68)	Some copies of first 1729 8° (seen in 1 copy of P779, 11 of P780)
NOTES:		Retouched (owl's head and talons; cover decorations of "Ogilby")
	No half title on reverse of leaf	All copies seen have half title 'THE | DUNCIAD.'
	Bottom of frame closed	Bottom of frame open

Appendix 3

the Altar Frontispiece

1.iii	1.iv	2
—	—	THE | DUNCI|AD
Gildon & Woolfton. ag.ˢᵗ Xʳ.	—	P. & K. ARTHUR
—	—	Shakesp. Reftor'd
—	—	OGIL|BY
—	Oldmix: Hift: of Stuartf	Dennis's Works
BLACK|MORE	—	NEW|CAS|TLE
—	—	Cibber's Plays
—	—	[absent]
Most copies of first 1729 8º (seen in 18 copies of P779, 22 of P780)	1735–36 8º (P785–86)	1728 "Gold chains" piracy (P769)
In P780 the plate faces the start of Book 1 or 2 of the poetic text	Retouched (upper cover of "Arthur"; lower serif of "d" in "Reftor'd" now curled upward)	
Half title present in 13 copies seen of P779, 6 of P780	No half title	No half title
Bottom of frame open	Bottom of frame open	Bottom of frame closed

APPENDIX 4

The 1728 Advertisement for
THE PROGRESS OF DULNESS

Page [52] of the first duodecimo impression of the 1728 *Dunciad* (*Foxon* P764); reproduced from a copy at Cornell University (Rare PR3625.A1 1728a) by permission of the Cornell University Library. The dimensions of the type page are 52 × 73 mm; the leaf measures 174 × 100 mm.

Speedily will be Published

The PROGRESS OF DULNESS,

AN

Historical POEM

By an Eminent Hand.

Price 1s. 6d.

APPENDIX 5

Annotations in the 1728 Huntington DUNCIAD

Although, as I have suggested in the consideration of Richardson's annotations, the Huntington copy of the 1728 octavo (RB 106517) appears to record changes Pope made for editions subsequent to 1728, some puzzles remain. To help resolve those questions, I here place those notes on record, with grateful acknowledgment to the Huntington Library, San Marino, California, for permission to do so. The presentation is based on the system outlined by Fredson Bowers in "Transcription of Manuscripts: The Record of Variants," *Studies in Bibliography* 29 (1976): 212–64. The list employs several abbreviations: del[eted], interl[ined], marg[inal], underl[ined], vert[ical]. The form of the eighteenth-century symbol for the word 'the' varies in the original; I have consistently transcribed 'y' with a cap as 'y^e'. A delta in the text appears to signify a deletion in later editions, and a marginal 'x' an alteration. As in the other Appendixes, page and line numbers follow the 1728 octavo *Dunciad* reproduced in the facsimile, and I have not distinguished the long ess.

These notes and marks correspond only in part with the sections that Richardson described as "torn out" of the manuscript when he annotated the Berg copy. The missing passages are approximately as follows: 1.73–224; 2.105–71, 245–316, 377–82 (end); 3.185–206, 217–86 (end).

Appendix 5

Title

Head	'[N. All here added or changd is from a Copy of Mr Popes of this same Edition.] Jonat. Richardson jun. Queen's Sq. *1777*' [*signature and address in different ink*]
Foot	'Mem. This was the first Edition of this Poem in England. There was another in Ireland after it, very incorrect, ye same year.'

Book 1

2.16f	*marg. caret and* 'The Inscription of [y]^e Poem to D^r· Swift added here since this Edit.'
6.94	*marg.* 'x' *and* 'And all ye mighty Mad in Dennis rage.'
7.116	[W]att[s] *interl.; marg.* 'x Withers, Quarles & Bloom.'
9.163	'pen' *underl.; marg.* 'Quill'
10.178	'His' *underl.; marg.* 'That'
11.191	'go,' *underl.; marg.* 'run'
11.192	'did grow' *underl.; marg.* 'begun'

Book 2

15.before 1	*marg. caret and* 'Twelve Verses added to ye beginning of this book in ye subsequent editions.'
19.73	*marg.* 'x'
20.93	*underl.; marg. delta, period*
20.94f	*interl.* 'Light fly diverse'
20.95	'Songs Sonnets Epigrams y^e ⸳' *below del.* 'His papers all, the sportive'

Appendix 5

Book 2

20.96	'Evans' *below* 'G———'; 'and' *below* 'to'
21.121	'the Goddess' *underl.; marg.* 'she gave him'
21.123	'Gives him' *underl.; marg.* 'A shaggy'
22.140–41	*marg. delta, vert. line*
22.143	'fair' *underl.*
23.157	*underl., except semicolon; marg.* 'The Wild Mæander washd ye Artists face'
23.159	*second* 'i' *of* 'Spirits' *del.*
27.234	'r' *above del. third* 't' *of* 'attempted'
29.275–76	*marg.* 'x', *vert. line, delta*
29.277	*marg.* 'x'
29.278	*marg.* 'x'
30.281	*marg.* 'x'
30.282	*marg.* 'x'
34.369	*marg.* 'x'
34.370	*marg.* 'x'
34.371	*marg.* 'x'

Book 3

41.97	*marg.* 'x'
41.98	*marg.* 'x'
44.153	'[*H*]eywood' *interl.*
44.154	'[*H*]orne[*ck*'s] *interl.*; '[*M*]itchel['s] *interl.*
44.155	*marg.* 'x'; 'Jacob' *above* 'W———n'; 'Grammar' *above* 'Scripture'
44.156	'Nor less revere him' *above* 'And mighty J———b'
45.159–60	*marg. vert. line, delta, period*
45.167	*marg.* 'x'
45.169	*marg.* 'x'

Appendix 5

Book 3

45.171	*marg.* 'x'
46.179	*marg.* 'x'
46.180	*marg.* 'x'
46.183	*marg.* 'x'
47.202	*marg.* 'x'
49.246	'some' *above underl.* 'the'
51.275	*marg.* 'x'
51.276	*marg.* 'x'
51.277	*marg.* 'x'
51.278	*marg.* 'x'
51.279–80	*marg.* 'x'
51.281–82	*marg. vert. line*
51.283	*marg.* 'x'
51.285	*marg.* 'x'

Index

Addison, Joseph, 60
Allibone, Samuel A., 17n
Anderson Auction Co., 44
Arbuthnot, John, *Three Hours after Marriage*, 7 n. 8
Atterbury, Francis, 30

Bentley, Richard, 47
Bettenham, James: acquaintance with Pope, 30; prints *Dunciad*, 30, 33, 35, 38, 49, 143, 156–57, 161; enters *Dunciad* in *Stationers' Register*, 18, 31
Blackmore, Sir Richard, 36, 39
Boileau-Despréaux, Nicolas, 48
Bolingbroke, Henry St. John, Lord, 15
Boswell, James, 23
Bowers, Fredson, 166
Bowles, William Lisle, 26
Bowyer, William, 30
Broome, William, xii n. 3
Buckley, Samuel, 34n
Burnet, Thomas, 60
Butt, John, 43 n. 23

Carruthers, Robert, xi
Caryll, John, 6
Catalogue of Prints and Drawings in the British Museum, 36n, 49n
Chalmers, John, 30n
Chandler, W. K., 33
Chauncy, Charles, 41, 42, 43, 44
Chauncy, Charles Snell, 42
Chauncy, Nathaniel, 42, 44
Christie, Manson and Woods, 43
Cibber, Colley, 26, 36
Codrus (Roman poet), 8; nickname for Elkanah Settle, 7, 8

Collating machines, xiv, 33, 34, 143
Cooke, Thomas, 20
Courthope, William John, 27, 42–43
Croker, John Wilson, 17 n. 13
Cromwell, Henry, 13, 36
Crowell, Thomas Y., 27
Curll, Edmund, xii n. 2, 13, 30, 55; *Compleat Key to the Dunciad*, 20–22, 156; *Curliad*, 21; *Laus Ululae*, 37; *Miscellanea*, 36–37

Daily Journal, xii n. 2, 15, 18
Daily Post, 19
Davis, Herbert, 27–28
Dennis, John, 8, 36, 39, 49; "A Letter against Mr. P. at large," 15; *Remarks upon . . . the Dunciad*, 49; *Reflections . . . Upon . . . An Essay Upon Criticism*, 12
de Ricci, Seymour, 42
Dilke, C. W., 17 n. 13
Dodd, Ann (wife and mother), 17, 17–18 n. 14, 36, 38
Dodd, Ann (daughter), 18n
Dodd, Nathaniel (husband and father), 18n
Dodd, Nathaniel, 18n
Dryden, John, 29–30; *Absalom and Achitophel*, 21; *MacFlecknoe*, 8
Duckett, George, 60
Dulness, 5–7, 15–16, 36–37
Dunciad, The: bawdiness in, 60; classical allusions in, 7, 8, 18, 23, 60, 61–62; keys to, 20–22; names in, 8, 11, 22, 24–25, 29–30, 36, 38–39, 52–53, 59, 156–57, 161; notes in, 55, 152; political satire in, 7, 22, 59–

171

Index

Dunciad, The (cont.)
  60; scatology in, 7; title of, 15–16; see also Physical features
  copies: Berg (1728), xiii, xiv, 41–43, 143, 166; Berg (1736), xiii, 41–42, 44; British Library, 22; Cornell, 164; Huntington, 41–42, 44–45, 58–59, 166; number examined, xiv, 143
  Dunciad Variorum (4°, 1729): planned, 11, 15, 18, 23, 56; changed from 1728 edition, xii, 21, 23–24; notes in, 8, 9, 11, 13 n. 11, 30, 36; dedicated to Swift, 15, 23, 58; printed and published, xin, 38, 49; presented to king, 20; used for later editions, 25–27; relationship to Richardson's annotations, 50–59, 166
  first edition (1728): method of composition, 3–4; early verses in, 4–7; Lord Mayor's Day setting, 7–9; Swift's contribution, 9–12; stimulation by attacks, 12–14; final drafts, 14–16; publication, xi, 16–18, 31; priority of editions, 29–30; relationship of impressions, 31–35; responses, 16–23; see also Physical features
  manuscripts: early, 9; First Broglio, 41–43, 48–49, 60; Second Broglio, 41, 49–58, 60; relationship of Broglios, 51–58; date of Richardson's collations, 48; literary significance, 59–61
  other editions: "Gold chains" (1728), 21, 30, 38, 156–57, 161; Dublin booksellers (1728), 20, 29–30, 156–57; first 8° Variorum (1729), 38–39, 51, 161; second 8° Variorum (1729), 25, 51, 161; Variorum (1735), 39, 51, 161; Variorum (1736), 39, 41–42, 44, 48, 51, 56–57; New Dunciad (1742), 25, 59; Four Books (1743), 26, 28, 55; type facsimile (1928), xii, 27; see also Dunciad, The: Dunciad Variorum (4°, 1729), and Pope, Alexander: collected editions

Elwin, Whitwell, 42–43
Elzevier editions, 35

Eusden, Laurence, 8
Evening-Post, 20

Fenton, Elijah, xii n. 3
F. G., 37n
Fielding, Henry, 7 n. 7; Covent-Garden Journal, 17–18 n. 14, 22–23
Fourdrinier, Paul, 37
Foxon, David, 4 n. 4, 17, 21, 30, 33, 35–36, 38

Garth, Samuel, Dispensary, 21
Gaskell, Philip, 155
Gay, John, 16, 17; Three Hours after Marriage, 7 n. 8
Gent, Thomas, 18n
George I (king of England), 37
George II (king of England), 20, 37
Gildon, Charles, 10, 39
Gilliver, Lawton, 38
Goldgar, Bertrand A., 18n
Greg, W. W., 27
Griffith, R. H., 17 n. 13, 30, 32–35, 42n
Grant, Francis, 44
Grolier Club, 43 n. 24, 44
Grundy, Isobel M., 7 n. 7
Guerinot, Joseph, xii, 12, 17, 19n

Harvey, Francis, 43
Heartman, Charles F., 45
Hill, George Birkbeck, xin
Hoe, Robert, 44–45
Homer, 18, 60
Horace, 61–62
Huntington, Henry E., 42n, 45
Huntington Library, 41, 44–45, 48, 58–59, 166

Jervas, Charles, 37
Johnson, Samuel, xin, 23

Kent, William, 37

Lees, W. Nassau, 43
Leranbaum, Miriam, 50
Lewis, William, 20
Lewis Walpole Library, 37n
Lord Mayor's Day, 7–8
Lounsbury, Thomas, 32, 34n

Index

Macaulay, Thomas Babington, 29
Mack, Maynard, xiii, 5n, 13, 13n, 50, 54, 55, 59, 64
McKenzie, Alan T., 36n
McLaverty, James, 50
Maevius, 10
Maittaire, Michael, 35, 52–53
Mengel, Elias F., Jr., 36n, 38
Milton, John, *Paradise Lost*, 35, 47
Mist's Weekly Journal, 20
Montagu, Lady Mary Wortley, 7 n. 7; *A Popp upon Pope*, 19
Motte, Benjamin, 14

Negus, Samuel, 30 n. 16
Newcastle, duchess of, 36, 39
New York Daily Tribune, 44
New York Herald, 44n
New York Sun, 44
New York Times, 44n
New York World, 44n
Nichols, John, 30
Notes and Queries, 29

Ogilby, John, 36
Oldmixon, John, 39
Ovid, *Metamorphoses*, 60
Oxford, Edward Harley, 2d earl of, 14, 17, 20, 52–53
Oxford University Press, 27

Persius, 60
Philips, Ambrose, 10
Physical features
    annotations, manuscript: ink, variations in, xiii–xiv, 58, 61–62; organization of, 62–63; overwriting in, 61, 62; pencil, use of, 61–62; symbols used in, 63–64, 166
    blanks in names, 11, 20–21, 24–25, 29–30, 58, 59, 144, 157
    capitalization, 156–57
    collation formulas, 31
    footnotes, 152
    frontispiece, 36–39, 161
    imposition, work-and-turn, 31
    italics, 52
    layout, 35–36
    leaf size, xiv, 164
    ornaments, 30, 152–53
    paper, 154–55; two-sheet moulds for, 155

    press figures, 153–54
    running titles, 34–35
    signatures, 153
    type page, xiv
    variants, textual: within and between manuscripts, 7 n. 8, 51–53, 59, 60–61, 64; between manuscripts and prints, 7 n. 8, 47–64; within an impression, xiv, 143; between impressions, 32, 33–34, 143–44, 152; between editions, 51–53, 55, 56, 156–57; in frontispiece, 38–39, 161; in works other than *Dunciad*, 47–48, 59; recorded in Twickenham Ed., 27, 57, 144, 152
Pope, Alexander. See also: *Dunciad, The*
    attacks on: before *Dunciad*, xi–xii, 12–14, 15, 16; after *Dunciad*, 16–17, 18–19, 22
    collected editions: 2° and 4° *Works II* (1735), 4, 25, 37, 48, 51, 59; second 8° *Works* (1736), 26; "deathbed edition" (1743–44), 26; Warburton (1751), 23, 59n; Warton (1797, 1822), 26; Tourneisen (1803), 26; Bowles (1806), 26; London booksellers (1812), 26; Globe (1869), 27; Elwin-Courthope (1871–86), xiii, 27, 42–43; Crowell (1896), 27; Twickenham (1939–69), 4 n. 3, 21, 26–27, 43, 57, 144, 152; Oxford Standard Authors (1966), 27–28
    correspondence, 4; to Buckley, 34n; to Caryll, 6; to Cromwell, 13, 36; to Motte, 14; to Oxford, 14, 19, 20, 53; to Richardson, Sr., 48; to Sheridan, 10, 12; to Swift, 10, 11, 13, 14, 15, 16; to Wycherley, 5; from Bolingbroke, 15; from Oxford, 20; from Swift, 10, 11, 15, 16, 19–20
    other works: *Alcander, Prince of Rhodes*, 4, 7; *Daily Post*, advertisement in, 19; Epistles, 48, 59; "First Epistle of the Second Book of Horace," 4 n. 2; "First Satire of the Second Book of Horace," 42, 61; *Essay on Criticism*, 7 n. 8, 20, 36, 43, 47; *Essay on Man*, 37, 42, 43, 47, 48; *Essay on Man*, drawing for frontispiece of, 37; *Iliad* trans., 30; *Miscellanies*, xii, 3n, 9, 14, 16; *Odyssey* trans., xii, 37; *Peri Bathous*, xii, 15, 16; *Progress*

Index

Pope, Alexander, (*cont.*)
of Dulness, 15, 18, 34, 164; Shakespeare ed., 13–14; *Temple of Fame*, 15; *Three Hours after Marriage*, 7 n. 8; "To the Author of . . . Successio," 4, 5, 7; *The What D'ye Call It*, 15; *Windsor Forest*, 15; Wycherley revisions and ed., 5, 6
Popp upon Pope, A (Montagu?), 19
Post-Boy, 8n
Prior, Matthew, 14
Prince, Daniel, 30, 49

Rackett, Magdalen, 19
Ralph, James, *Sawney*, 17
Richardson, Jonathan, Jr.: artistic ability of, 37–38; collates *Dunciad*, xiii, 3, 7 n. 8, 9, 23, 41–42, 166; collates other Pope works, 47–48, 59; *Explanatory Notes . . . on Milton's Paradise Lost*, 47; his copies of Pope works, 41–45, 47–48, 166; *Richardsoniana*, 19, 47–48
Richardson, Jonathan, Sr., 7 n. 6, 10, 37–38, 47, 48; *Explanatory Notes on Milton's Paradise Lost*, 47
Rogers, Robert W., 8, 49–50
Rosenbach, A. S. W., 44
Rowe, Nicholas, 8
Ruffhead, Owen, 61

Savage, Richard, xi-xii, 17
Schmitz, Robert M., 7 n. 8
Scriblerus Club, 11
Settle, Elkanah, 8–9; "Eusebia Triumphans," 4, 7
Shakespeare, William, 60
Sherburn, George, 3–4, 7 n. 6, 8, 10–11, 48, 52
Sheridan, Thomas, 10, 12, 12n
Smith, George D., 44–45
Solly, Edward, 29
Sotheby's, 44
South, Robert, *Sermons*, 30 n. 17
Sparrow, Anthony, *Rational . . . Exposition of the Book of Common Prayer*, 30 n. 17
Spence, Joseph, 4, 9, 19

Spenser, Edmund, *Faerie Queene*, 9, 16
Stationer's Company, 18, 31
Stevens, B. F., 44
Stowe, Harriet Beecher, *Key to Uncle Tom's Cabin*, 25
Sutherland, James, 7 n. 7, 7 n. 8, 26–27, 43, 57, 60
Swift, Jonathan, 9, 22, 49, 56; correspondence, 10, 11, 12n, 13, 14, 15, 16, 19–20; dedication of *Dunciad* to, 15, 23, 58; "Dr. Sw—— to Mr. P——e," 3, 12; *Miscellanies*, xii, 3n, 9, 14
Szladits, Lola L., 43

Tangye, Richard, 44
Tanselle, G. Thomas, xivn
Theobald, Lewis, 11, 26, 36, 49; *Shakespeare Restored*, 13, 32; Wycherley ed., 5, 6
Thoms, William, 29, 33
Thorold, Sir George, 7
Tickell, Thomas, 15
Times Literary Supplement, 32
Tourneisen, J. J., 26
Tracy, Clarence, xin
Treadwell, J. Michael, 18n

Vander Meulen, David L., 35n
Virgil, 10, 18; *Aeneid*, 7, 60

Wakefield, Gilbert, 60
Walpole, Sir Robert, 20
Warburton, William, 59
Ward, A. W., 27
Warton, Joseph, 26
Watts, John, 35–36
Wimsatt, William K., 47n
Wise, Thomas J., 32–34
Woolston, Thomas, 39
Wycherley, William, 5n; *Miscellany Poems*, 5; "Panegyrick on Dulness," 5, 7; "To a Doctor of Physick," 6; *Works*, ed. Theobald, 5, 6; *Works*, ed. Pope, 5

Young, Edward, 15
Young, Owen D., 43, 44